NSTA PATHWAYS

To the Science Standards

Elementary School Edition

Editor
Lawrence F. Lowery

Second Edition

Guidelines for Moving the Vision into Practice

National Science Teachers Association

Claire Reinburg, Director
Judy Cusick, Associate Editor
Carol Duval, Associate Editor
Betty Smith, Associate Editor

Art and Design
Linda Olliver, Director
NSTA Web
Tim Weber, Webmaster
Periodicals Publishing
Shelley Carey, Director
Printing and Production
Catherine Lorrain-Hale, Director
Publications Operations
Erin Miller, Manager
sciLINKS
Tyson Brown, Manager
Marketing
Holly Hemphill, Director

National Science Teachers Association
Gerald F. Wheeler, Executive Director
David Beacom, Publisher

NSTA Press, NSTA Journals, and the NSTA Web site deliver high-quality resources for science educators.

NSTA Pathways to the Science Standards:
Guidelines for Moving the Vision into Practice
ELEMENTARY SCHOOL EDITION, Second Edition

Editor: Lawrence F. Lowery
Contributing Editors: Juliana Texley, Sheila Marshall, Ann Wild
Contributors: Charles Barman, Karen Bishop, Catherine Blair, Pat Bowers, Mike DiSpezio, Sheila Dunston, Jerry Foster, Carol Glass, Almeta Hall, Roger Johnson, Tricia Kerr, Mozell Lang, JoAnne de Maria, Joan Braunagel McShane, Suzanne Moore, Norma Nealy, Karen Ostlund, Michael Padilla, Larry Schafer, Juliana Texley, Gerry Wheeler, BonitaTalbot-Wiley, Deborah Wilson, and the NSTA Committee on Preschool-Elementary Science Teaching

Editor of the Facilities Section: Suzanne Lieblich
Contributors to the Facilities Section: James Biehle, LaMoine Motz, Victor Showalter, Sandra West,

NSTA Project Manager: Sheila Marshall
NSTA Editorial Assistant: Christopher Hampton
NSTA project editors for the second edition: Jessica Green and Erin Miller

NSTA is grateful for the generous contributions by Monsanto Fund, DuPont, American Petroleum Institute, and Chemical Manufacturers Association that made this effort possible.

NSTA would like to thank the National Research Council of the National Academy of Sciences for permission to reprint material that originally appeared in the National Science Education Standards *(Washington, DC: National Academy Press, © 1996)*

Book Design: Dragon Graphics
Cover: Elinor Allen, Allen and Associates, Ltd. Washington, DC
Cover Photographs: Left: Presidential Awards, Center: Mike L. Shaw and Gregg F. Smith, Right: Eastman
Illustrations: Lana Dragon-Stire Walt

Stock Number: PB124X
ISBN Number: 0-87355-161-3
Printed in the U.S.A. by Automated Graphic Systems, Inc.

Table of Contents

About *sci*Links

NSTA Pathways to the Science Standards brings you *sci*LINKS, a new project that blends the two main delivery systems for curriculum—books and telecommunications—into a dynamic new educational tool for children, their parents, and their teachers. *sci*LINKS links specific science content with instructionally-rich Internet resources. *sci*LINKS represents an enormous opportunity to create new pathways for learners, new opportunities for professional growth among teachers, and new modes of engagement for parents.

In this *sci*LINKed text, you will find an icon —like the one on this page—that illustrates the concepts in the content standards for grades K–6. Under the icon, you will find the *sci*LINKS URL (http://www.scilinks.org/) and a code. Go to the *sci*LINKS Web site, sign in, type the code from your text, and you will receive a list of URLs that are selected by science educators.

Web sites are chosen for accurate and age-appropriate content and good pedagogy. The underlying database changes constantly, eliminating dead or revised sites or simply replacing them with better selections. The ink may dry on the page, but the science it describes will always be fresh.

*sci*LINKS also ensures that the online content teachers count on remains available for the life of this text. The *sci*LINKS search team regularly reviews the materials to which this text points—revising the URLs as needed or replacing Web pages that have disappeared with new pages. When you send your students to *sci*LINKS to use a code from this text, you can always count on good content being available.

The selection process involves four review stages:

1. A cadre of under-graduate science education majors searches the Web for interesting science resources. The under-graduates submit about 500 sites a week for consideration.

2. Packets of these Web pages are organized and sent to teacher-Web-watchers with expertise in given fields and grade levels. The teacher-Web-watchers can also submit Web pages that they have found on their own. The teachers pick the jewels from this selection and correlate them to the National Science Education Standards. These pages are submitted to the *sci*LINKS database.

3. Scientists review these correlated sites for accuracy.

4. NSTA staff approve the Web pages and edit the information provided for accuracy and consistent style.

*sci*LINKS is a free service for textbook and supplemental resource users, but obviously someone must pay for it. Participating publishers pay a fee to NSTA for each book that contains *sci*LINKS. The program is also supported by a grant from the National Aeronautics and Space Administration (NASA).

Introduction

I t is rare when a profession reaches national consensus in its vision for change. The National Science Education Standards represent just such a landmark effort. Science educators, scientists, administrators, businesspeople, and concerned citizens, coming from very different perspectives, have joined forces to speak eloquently for science education in our schools.

The very breadth of the Standards may seem intimidating at first—something for everyone—but nothing for tomorrow's lesson. So, for elementary teachers across America, we offer this practical guidebook, *NSTA Pathways to the Science Standards: Guidelines for Moving the Vision into Practice.*

In its pages, we demonstrate how you can carry the vision of the Standards—for teaching, professional development, assessment, content, program, and system—into the real world of your classroom and school. This book is also a tool for you to use in collaborating with principals, local and state administrators, parents, school board members, and other stakeholders in science education.

Pathways was created by an impressive partnership of teachers and administrators who believe that many elements of the Standards are already in place today. Great science education happens in many elementary classrooms, and today's teachers *can* achieve the teaching and

STEVE BUHMAN

learning detailed in these Standards now and in the coming decades.

Many Options, No One Way

In elementary schools nationwide, the Standards and the *NSTA Pathways* travel guide to the Standards will spark changes that will spring from the strengths of each school faculty and the unique character of each community. Because there is no one correct pathway to achieve the goals of the Standards, this *Pathways* book presents a variety of ways, through suggestions and models, to help elementary teachers begin to implement the Standards.

You can start by building on what works well today in your classroom and school. Several types of pilot projects and established programs that illustrate the vision of excellence can be found in many classrooms across the country. Depending on resources, commitment, and interest, each elementary teacher, each

school, and each community will follow a different pathway in reaching for the vision of the Standards.

Basic Principles in the Standards

All students can learn science, and all students should have the opportunity to become scientifically literate. This is one of the strongest of the four foundational themes of the National Science Education Standards. This effort must begin in the early grades when students are naturally curious about the world around them and eager to explore it. The essential experiences of science inquiry, exploration, and application must be provided to *every* student in the nation from kindergarten through grade 12.

Another strong theme in the Standards is that learning science is an active process. The Standards rest solidly on the foundation of educational research that demonstrates that learning is an active process achieved by

enthusiastic and motivated students. Much of the literature that supports this perspective uses the term "constructivism" to represent the student's role in building concepts.

Beginning the Journey

The primary strength of the National Science Education Standards is the process through which its vision was created: a consensus of divergent viewpoints forged of shared commitment. The document paints a clear picture of what should be taught (content standards), how to do it (teaching and program standards), how you will know when you get there (assessment standards), and how to build capacity for change (professional development and education system standards).

We invite you to use this book to design your own pathway for putting the National Science Education Standards into action in your classroom and school.

EMILY KING

How To Use This Book

This *NSTA Pathways to the Science Standards* has one audience—you, the elementary classroom teacher. As your guide to the National Science Education Standards, *Pathways* provides practical ideas for putting the vision of the Standards into action in your classroom.

The first three and last two chapters of the book discuss the Standards that apply to teachers of all grade levels: Teaching, Professional Development, Assessment, Program, and System Standards. In each of these chapters you will find a discussion of the Standards followed by Resources for the Road—a list of pertinent articles, most of them from *Science and Children* and *Science Scope*. You can access the NSTA-published articles on the *Re-*sources *for the Road CD-ROM* that is available as a supplement to this book. Each of the five K–12 Standards ends with a Changing Emphases chart.

It is important to remember that efforts toward change and improvement in each of the five Standards areas mentioned above must occur if the students are to achieve the Content Standards. As the Standards point out, elementary teachers are not expected to be the *sole* agents of change. The effort requires the support of principals, local and state administrators, parents, legislators, volunteers, business representatives, and interested citizens working together.

The fourth chapter of *Pathways* examines the science goals for elementary students as outlined in the Content Standards. Because U.S. elementary schools still include grade 5, and most have not moved grade 6 into the middle school, this book focuses on content goals defined in the Standards for the elementary grades (K–4) as well as the goals defined for the middle school (grades 5–8) that are appropriate for grades 5 and 6.

The Content Standards chapter includes a general discussion (together with a fold-out section on the back cover of the book) about the learning capabilities of students in the various grade levels. This is followed by discussions of selected content areas with practical suggestions, including assessment options, for bringing the specific content area into your classroom. Vignettes—called

"A Classroom in Action"—are presented as examples of how some of the Standards might be implemented, using a variety of approaches adaptable to many different settings.

Three of the sections will be paired consistently with one of the icons on the right to help guide you through the Standards.

The book has five appendices, including a history of the Science Standards movement, a complete list of all the National Science Education Standards, recommendations for setting up an elementary science facility, a list of addresses for elementary science programs, and ways to adapt a science program for students with special needs.

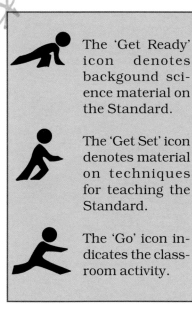

The 'Get Ready' icon denotes backgound science material on the Standard.

The 'Get Set' icon denotes material on techniques for teaching the Standard.

The 'Go' icon indicates the classroom activity.

Pathways is to use and to share. It will enable you to identify, create, and implement classroom experiences that will have power and value for your students and improve science learning in your classroom.

Pathways has key information that you can share with those who determine policy and make decisions at district and state levels. We encourage you to share this book with principals, local and state administrators, your board of education, policymakers, parents, business representatives, and other citizens to help them understand what is needed in your classroom to prepare your students for the 21st century.

Bon voyage! As you travel along, remember there are many pathways you can choose in reaching for the vision of the National Science Education Standards. Your journey will be an exciting one!

GWYN LOUD

Science Teaching Standards

As teachers, we are the most important force in the education system. We are the key to reform.

Realizing the Teaching Standards

As teachers, you are the most important component in the education system. You are the individuals who will chart the pathway toward implementing the National Science Education Standards in your classroom and school. How your students learn science depends on you. To assist you, the Standards suggest new ways to approach the teaching and learning of science.

First, they urge teachers to recognize that science is a discipline that must be taught to *every* student in *every* elementary school and that it must be taught using an inquiry/thinking approach. This means that science has an important place in the school curriculum. There is no legitimate reason to push science aside or relegate it to an end-of-the-day, isolated activity.

The Standards reassure teachers that they, like their students, are lifelong learners. The Standards offer ideas for becoming more expert whether you currently teach science with confidence or whether you feel uncomfortable teaching science.

Becoming an Expert

The Standards urge teachers to set higher personal standards for their instruction and to become expert at
- facilitating ideas as students investigate individually or in collaborative groups
- budgeting time, allowing inquiries to be explored and not cut off by a ringing bell
- assessing progress by observing students, asking effective questions, and evaluating written work (both formally and infor-

mally), thereby determining what changes need to occur to improve instruction and learning
- allowing students to inquire, explore, and experiment in depth over days and perhaps weeks
- providing and maintaining materials and equipment for students to use in collaborating with colleagues

For the complete text of the National Science Education Standards, see Appendix B.

Both the Teaching Standards and the Content Standards put high value on

ANGELA NICKEL

"inquiry" as an important component of both science teaching and science learning. Inquiry is a natural process in which individuals ask questions, gather information through many and varied activities, examine data, and develop explanations about that data to answer the original question. Inquiry is basic to science itself—it is how scientists work. Giving students opportunities to inquire is a vital component in helping them become scientifically literate.

Although all children have the capacity to inquire, that capacity changes and becomes more sophisticated as children mature and gain experience. Very young children, for example, tend to explore the answer to a question through trial-and-error tests. Older children explore questions with trial-and-error experiences/experiments and are introduced to testing by learning about variables and establishing controls. It is important, then, that teachers become expert at facilitating quality inquiry experiences appropriate for the students they teach. To do this, teachers must use their knowledge of child development and their familiarity with the learning characteristics and styles of their students. Teachers must provide the appropriate classroom setting for students to carry out inquiry investigations if the best possible science learning is to occur. Ideas and suggestions for various grade levels are provided in the Content Standards chapter.

Constructing Their Own Knowledge

Ideas for improving the teaching and learning of science grew from a body of research that permeates the National Science Education Standards and the current science education reform movement.

We now know that children don't learn simply by listening to someone talk or by reading a book. In other words, we cannot just transfer, or hand over, our own understanding of the natural world to children. We cannot just show and tell. As the Standards point out, students have to construct, or build, their *own* knowledge in "a process that is individual and social." Students have to take an active role in their own learning. This teaching/learning relationship is called constructivism.

Research strongly supports the idea that children learn best by building their own knowledge through appropriate concrete experiences. Because students acquire knowledge at different paces and through different learning styles, teachers need to provide instruction that is flexible and sensitive to these differences.

It is important that teachers choose thoughtfully what they want their students to learn. They should engage students in ideas that are relevant to the learner and ideas that are likely to serve the student

STEVE BUHMAN

well over a lifetime. It is also important to recognize that not all hands-on experiences are constructive experiences. Recipe-type experiences, in which students follow directions to replicate an experiment or build a model, are not constructive experiences. Experiences without science content (for example, sorting M&M's by color), are not constructive science experiences. One-time activities are also not constructive experiences.

ANN FLOYD

Helping Students Learn

The role of teachers is to help students build accurate concepts, use process skills, and reject incorrect ideas. Teachers can engage students, structure time, create a setting, make tools available, identify resources, assess students' progress, and guide students' self-assessment.

Here is how you can apply the constructivist approach:

- *Begin by Assessing Student Preconceptions.* Until you know what preconceptions and knowledge students have about a topic, building new ideas will be difficult. Interviews, questions, drawings, predictions, and group discussions can help uncover preconceptions.
- *Build on past experience.* Meaning is created in a student's mind when concrete, physical experiences interact with existing beliefs. When an experience contradicts prior knowledge, the child may become

surprised, frustrated—and more eager to learn.
- *Take Sufficient Time.* Acquiring new knowledge can only happen if a student is given unhurried experiences and the motivation to allow learning to happen.
- *Foster Continuing Inquiry.* Through questioning, self-assessment, and open-ended investigations, constructivist teachers provide environments that challenge students to learn.

Asking Questions

Good questions excite and motivate children. Good questions are open-ended—they don't have one right answer. Open-ended questions might ask, "What if?"; "What do you think will happen next?"; "What do you think we should do?"; and "Can you tell me more about that? Teachers asking open-ended questions avoid questions that have only

"yes" or "no" answers and questions that rely on quick memory recall.

When students are asked open-ended questions, they will pose innovative questions of their own, thus expanding their own capacity for creative thinking and problem-solving. Teachers learn about students through the answers they give, but even more from the questions they ask.

Learning to ask, pace, and interpret good questions are vital skills in classrooms where the Standards guide science learning. Good questions support inquiry, provide ongoing assessment of student progress, and can be used to guide the pace of instruction.

Science for All

Children differ in many ways, and teachers need to adjust

An Example

One day students were discussing a high wire performer they had seen at the circus. Several students wondered how someone learned to be a high wire performer. One girl said, "You know it takes terrific balance!" Someone else commented, "Just what is balance, anyway?" The first girl said, "Let's find out!"

So she started to investigate the scientific concept of balance. As she tried to balance a cut-out figure upright on the end of her finger, she actively carried out the process of inquiry. She asked "what-if" questions and then tried out various arrangements, moving the figure forward or backward on her finger, adding clay as weight to different parts of the cut-out. She described what she was doing, shared her thoughts with the other students, and listened to what they suggested. The teacher and the other children asked questions throughout the investigation. The students also read some reference material about balance and high wire circus performers. Little by little, the students moved closer to finding an answer to the class' questions. In this example, the students freely explored how an object balances, first constructing an intuitive notion about a particular kind of balance.

their instruction to meet students where they are. In your classroom there will inevitably be students with various learning styles; from different racial, ethnic, and cultural backgrounds; and with a variety of special needs.

How can teachers support diverse learners in their classrooms while working to build a real community of learners? First, by modeling acceptance and tolerance themselves. Second, by consciously choosing methods and assessments that support individual learning styles. And, third, by recognizing that much learning occurs during the interactions of students with one another and with the teacher.

Appendix E has more information on adjusting classroom instruction for *all* students.

Six Teaching Standards

In addition to promoting the use of inquiry and the constructivist approach in science teaching, the Standards address other teaching-related issues relevant to effective practice. The Standards envision elementary teachers becoming more expert at

- selecting or planning an inquiry-based science program for their students
- guiding and facilitating science learning
- engaging in ongoing assessment of his or her teaching and of student learning
- designing and managing learning environments that

provide students with the time, space, and resources needed for learning science
- developing communities of science learners that reflect the intellectual rigor of scientific inquiry and the social values conducive to science learning
- participating actively in the ongoing planning and development of their school science program

For a complete list of all the National Science Education Standards, see Appendix C.

Filling in the Gaps

To carry out the goals of these Standards, teachers themselves must continue to be students of human learning, science subject matter, and pedagogy. Expert teachers are knowledgeable in all three domains.

A teacher need not be a professional scientist to be a quality teacher of elementary science, but he or she needs to be scientifically literate and have the interest to continue learning more and more science. The Standards stress that quality teaching involves knowledge in each domain as well as skill at blending that knowledge through effective teaching strategies.

Andersen, Hans O. (1991, May). Y'all Can. *Science Scope, 14* (8), 28–31.

Armstrong, Thomas. (1994). *Multiple Intelligences in the Classroom*. Alexandria, VA: Association for Supervision and Curriculum Development (ASCD).

Bellamy, Nedaro. (1994, March). Bias in the Classroom: Are We Guilty? *Science Scope, 17* (6), 60–63.

Blosser, Patricia E. (1991). *How To Ask the Right Questions*. Arlington, VA: National Science Teachers Association (NSTA).

Burgreen, Sid. (1995, September). How to Annoy Students and Influence Contest Judges. *Science and Children, 33* (1), 28–30.

Campbell, Melvin, and **Burton, VirLynn**. (1994, April). Learning in Their Own Style. *Science and Children, 31* (7), 22–24, 39.

Carey, Shelley Johnson (Ed.). (1993). *Science for All Cultures*. Arlington, VA: National Science Teachers Association (NSTA).

Chahrour, Janet. (1994, October). Perfecting the Question. *Science Scope, 18* (2), 9–11.

Hampton, Elaine, and **Gallegos, Charles**. (1994, March). Science for All Students. *Science Scope, 17* (6), 5–6, 7.

Hausfather, Samuel J. (1992, November/December). It's Time for Conceptual Change: A Flexible Approach Leads to Understanding. *Science and Children, 30* (3), 22–23.

Hinton, Nadine K. (1994, February). The Pyramid Approach to Reading, Writing, and Asking Questions. *Science Scope, 17* (5), 44–46.

Ivy, Tamra. (1994, March). Turning an Educator's Vision into a Classroom Reality. *Science Scope, 17* (6), 10–14.

Johnson, Janice K. (1991, October). On Research: Focus on Pre-reading Activities To Improve Student Reading Comprehension. *Science Scope, 15* (2), 32–34.

Keys, Carolyn W. (1996, February). Inquiring Minds Want To Know. *Science Scope, 19* (5), 17–19.

Koch, Janice. (1993, March). Face to Face with Science Misconceptions. *Science and Children, 30* (3), 39–40.

Kulas, Linda Lingenfelter. (1995, January). I Wonder.... *Science and Children, 32* (4), 16–18, 32.

Leach, Lisa S. (1994, March). Sexism in the Classroom: A Self-Quiz for Teachers. *Science Scope, 17* (6), 54–59.

Liggitt-Fox, Dianna. (1997, February). Fighting Student Misconceptions: Three Effective Strategies. *Science Scope, 20* (5), 28–30.

Ossont, Dave. (1993, May). How I Use Cooperative Learning. *Science Scope, 16* (8) 28–31.

Padilla, Michael J., and **Pyle, Eric J**. (1996, May). Observing and Inferring Promotes Science Learning. *Science and Children, 33* (8), 22–25.

Pearlman, Susan, and **Pericak-Spector, Kathleen**. (1992, October). Expect the Unexpected Question. *Science and Children, 30* (2), 36–37.

Rezba, Richard J., Cothron, Julia H., and **Giese, Ronald N**. (1992, February). Traditional Labs + New Questions = Improved Student Performance. *Science Scope, 15* (5), 39–44.

Roth, Wolff-Michael, and **Bowen, Michael**. (1993, January). Maps for More Meaningful Learning. *Science Scope, 16* (4), 24–25.

Roth, Wolff-Michael, and **Verechaka, Guennadi**. (1993, January). Plotting a Course with Vee Maps. *Science and Children, 30* (4), 24–27.

Rowe, Mary Budd. (1996, September). Science, Silence, and Sanctions. *Science and Children, 34* (1), 35–37, 34.

Schulte, Paige L. (1996, November/December). A Definition of Constructivism. *Science Scope, 20* (3), 25–27.

Simons, Grace H., and **Hepner, Nancy**. (1992, September). The Special Student in Science. *Science Scope, 16* (1), 34–39, 54.

Stepans, Joseph, and **Veath, M. Lois**. (1994, May). How Do Students Really Explain Changes in Matter? *Science Scope, 17* (8), 31–35.

Sumrall, William J. (1997, January). Why Avoid Hands-On Science? *Science Scope, 20* (4), 16–19.

Watson, Scott B. (1992, February). Cooperative Methods. *Science and Children, 29* (5), 30–31, 47.

The full text to most of these resources is available on NSTA's supplementary *Resources for the Road* CD-ROM.

Changing Emphases

The National Science Education Standards envision change throughout the system. The Teaching Standards encompass the following changes in emphases:

LESS EMPHASIS ON	MORE EMPHASIS ON
Treating all students alike and responding to the group as a whole	Understanding and responding to individual student's interests, strengths, experiences, and needs
Rigidly following curriculum	Selecting and adapting curriculum
Focusing on student acquisition of information	Focusing on student understanding and use of scientific knowledge, ideas, and inquiry processes
Presenting scientific knowledge through lecture, text, and demonstration	Guiding students in active and extended scientific inquiry
Asking for recitation of acquired knowledge	Providing opportunities for scientific discussion and debate among students
Testing students for factual information at the end of the unit or chapter	Continuously assessing student understanding
Maintaining responsibility and authority	Sharing responsibility for learning with students
Supporting competition	Supporting a classroom community with cooperation, shared responsibility, and respect
Working alone	Working with other teachers to enhance the science program

Reprinted with permission from the *National Science Education Standards.* © 1996 National Academy of Sciences. Courtesy of the National Academy Press, Washington, D.C.

NINA GUTHRIE

MIKE DONALDSON

Professional Development Standards

The Standards challenge us to become dedicated, lifelong learners.

Reaching for the Professional Development Standards

BOB STOCKFIELD

Professional development is a career-long endeavor. No matter the field (medicine, law, teaching), a degree does not make one an excellent practitioner. Experience certainly helps, but continual learning must be a major career commitment for all professionals, including teachers of every grade level.

The Standards urge elementary teachers to become lifelong learners so that they can expand their knowledge of science content and learning theories, thus becoming more skilled at pedagogy and inquiry.

According to the Standards, professional development for teachers of science requires

• learning essential science content through the perspectives and methods of inquiry

• integrating knowledge of science, learning, pedagogy, and students, and applying that knowledge to science learning

- building understanding and the ability for lifelong learning
- professional development programs that are coherent and integrated

Setting Personal Goals

The Professional Development Standards (for the full text, see Appendix B) challenge each teacher to set personal goals for professional development. The Standards put the responsibility for achieving these goals squarely on the shoulders of teachers. Professional development is not the responsibility of administrators, school boards, or school systems and districts, although these groups *must* make significant contributions to science education, including supporting teachers' efforts in professional development.

For many teachers who have been conditioned to expect their district to provide the professional development program, the Standards set new expectations. (It may also be new to school administrators who have assumed that a staff inservice was the best inservice possible!)

The Professional Development Standards relate to what teachers need to know about science and learning and how they effectively transfer that knowledge to teaching. Clearly the intent of these Standards cannot be accomplished in a one-day inservice workshop. The learning will span an entire career.

Understanding Science

The first two Professional Development Standards describe the essential content and elements of teaching. Adequate content is described as a "broad base of understanding" in both science disciplines and learning theory.

Elementary teachers of grades K-4 are expected to have a broad knowledge of science content, with some in-depth experiences in one of the science disciplines. Teachers of grades 5 and 6 should also have a broad understanding of science content but are also expected to be familiar with at least one sci-ence discipline. All elementary teachers need to know how to use the process of inquiry, how content knowledge is attained, and how to use science process skills. The essence of science is not the content alone, but the process of inquiry through which the content was derived.

Another way to say it is that knowledge is not simply what we know, but how we come to know it. For example, it may be interesting to know the distance to a planet or star (a content fact), but it is even more interesting and appropriate from a science viewpoint to know how the human mind found out how to measure that distance without being able to travel it.

DONALD DAVIS

Understanding Learning

The Standards support the growing body of research on learning theory. Because we now know that learning is not passive, teachers need to develop expertise in more than just conveying knowledge verbally.

Teachers need to know how children learn—cognitively, socially, and psychologically—so that they can adjust their instruction to meet different developmental capabilities and different learning styles of their students. This knowledge is critical for making decisions about what to teach, how to pace instruction, and how to select, adapt, or create appropriate curriculum and instructional activities wisely.

Teachers also need to develop expertise in knowing the difference between pseudoscience hands-on activities and authentic science hands-on activities. They need proficiency in asking questions, guiding discussions, and organizing students into cooperative and collaborative groupings. They need skill in assessing what students know and what they can do.

What's New?

Professional development programs in the 1990s look different from the programs teachers have known in the past. According to Sparks (1995), today's programs are focused on schools, not districts, and concentrate on student needs (not adult needs). Professional activities let teachers themselves study rather than turning tasks over to "visiting experts." Staff developers serve as facilitators, not trainers. Staff development is seen as indispensable, as in every profession, and thus no longer considered a frill.

Choose Your Pathway

There are many pathways for you to take as you work toward achieving the Professional Development Standards. Here are a few of them:

Graduate Courses

One of the most common routes to improve knowledge is enrolling in graduate courses. Some of these courses provide opportunities for additional learning in the laboratory, in research, and in teaching skills. They often provide discussions about why some strategies work well in classrooms. Many colleges and universities give teachers the opportunity to design individual programs around a set of courses to work toward an advanced degree.

Structured Inservice Programs

Today many school systems allow staff committees to design department, building, or district inservice programs. Some local resources, such as science centers, museums, and industries, plan programs specifically for classroom teachers. Teachers attending these programs in teams, accompanied by a school administrator, become more effective in transferring what they have learned to the school setting. The most effective staff development programs are long-range (not one-shot workshops) that model the information.

Professional Associations

Thousands of teachers attend national and regional conferences sponsored by professional associations. NSTA sponsors one national and three regional conventions on science education/teaching each year. For the cost of registration, teachers can select from hundreds of workshops. In addition, the exhibits are expansive, and there are numerous opportunities to network with other teachers.

(Choose your Pathway (Cont'd))

Journals

Membership in a professional association makes available professional journals (such as *Science and Children* and *Science Scope* from NSTA), newspapers, and newsletters that bring classroom science ideas and news to your doorstep.

Collaboration with Other Professionals

Teaching is no longer a private endeavor. Collaboration and team teaching are enriching instruction. Non-threatening coaching by a fellow teacher of science can offer additional opportunities to discover other styles, strategies, and options in teaching science. Mentoring (whether formal or informal) is another form of collaboration that opens the door for giving and receiving feedback about the teaching and learning that occurs in classrooms.

Self-Reflection and Inquiry

Not all learning experiences need to involve structured meetings, nor do they need to be group-oriented. There is much value in reading, studying, and exploring on your own. In fact, an important component of any career-long professional development plan must be self-reflective inquiry activities. As we try new ideas, we might use journals, audiotapes, and videotapes to track our progress.

Evaluation

Using evaluation as a vehicle for professional development will seem strange to most teachers. New, more reflective systems for evaluation can become valuable opportunities for teachers to talk with another educator about classroom decisions involving curriculum, delivery, and climate. If evaluation is to be a tool for growth, however, teachers must be full partners in developing the evaluation system.

School Improvement for Professional Growth

Setting common goals can provide a school- or district-wide impetus for professional development. A shared direction (such as redesigning the science program) can prompt a group to determine what strategy or plan has the best hope of success. Most plans include regular evaluation of progress. Having a voice in the policies and procedures that affect their classrooms will certainly increase teachers' sense of ownership and dedication.

Other Possibilities

Internships in industry or research provide new perspectives for science teachers. Travel (either to scientific sites or to other classrooms) has long been considered one of the most motivating professional development resources.

Closer to home, exploration of the World Wide Web, including the NSTA web site at http://www.nsta.org/ or online networks, can yield a wealth of resources and the opportunity to find answers to questions and share ideas with colleagues.

The possibilities for professional development are limitless. The critical question is "How does this experience move me toward my personal goal of becoming the best teacher I can be?"

ERIC, U.S. Department of Education. Professional Development. (Theme Issue) (1995, Winter). *ERIC Review, 3* (3),1-32.

Mason, Cheryl. (1993). *Preparing and Directing a Teacher Institute.* Arlington, VA: National Science Teachers Association (NSTA).

Massell, Laura Nault, and **Searles, Georgiana M.** (1995, February). An Alliance for Science. *Science and Children, 32* (5), 22-25.

National Science Teachers Association (NSTA). (1992). *NSTA Standards for Science Teacher Preparation.* Arlington, VA: Author. Adopted by the National Council for Accreditation of Teacher Education (NCATE).

Rodrigue, Polly, and **Tingle, Joy B.** (1994, January). The Extra Step: Linking Inservice and Preservice Teachers. *Science and Children, 31* (4), 34-36.

Sparks, Dennis. (1995, Winter). A Paradigm Shift in Staff Development. In Professional Development. (Theme Issue). *ERIC Review, 3* (3), 2-4.

Voyles, Martha, and **Charnetski, Deborah.** (1994, March). A Powerful Partnership. *Science and Children, 31* (6), 25-27, 46.

The full text to most of these resources is available on NSTA's supplementary *Resources for the Road CD-ROM.*

Changing Emphases

The National Science Education Standards envision change throughout the system. The Professional Development Standards encompass the following changes in emphases:

LESS EMPHASIS ON	MORE EMPHASIS ON
Transmission of teaching knowledge and skills by lectures	Inquiry into teaching and learning
Learning science by lecture and reading	Learning science through investigation and inquiry
Separation of science and teaching knowledge	Integration of science and teaching knowledge
Separation of theory and practice	Integration of theory and practice in school settings
Individual learning	Collegial and collaborative learning
Fragmented, one-shot sessions	Long-term coherent plans
Courses and workshops	A variety of professional development activities
Reliance on external expertise	Mix of internal and external expertise
Staff developers as educators	Staff developers as facilitators, consultants, and planners
Teacher as technician	Teacher as intellectual, reflective practitioner
Teacher as consumer of knowledge about teaching	Teacher as producer of knowledge about teaching
Teacher as follower	Teacher as leader
Teacher as an individual based in a classroom	Teacher as member of a collegial professional community
Teacher as target of change	Teacher as source and facilitator of change

Assessment Standards

Assessment isn't the final step in education—it's the first.

Exploring the Assessment Standards

Although there is a great deal of discussion about new types of assessments in elementary science, this need not be intimidating because the majority of elementary teachers already have the tools they need to improve classroom assessment. Like the cart and horse, teaching and assessment are inseparable partners. Elementary teachers have a special understanding of their students. Unconsciously and consciously, they make decisions about student progress as they move around the classroom: "She knows it; he needs more practice." This is assessment while teaching.

All well-designed science programs have a plan that enables teachers to determine how well each student is doing. There are two very different approaches to designing this plan. The most common and traditional approach relies on evaluation procedures, the other on assessment procedures.

Evaluations compare and rank what students have learned at a specific time, usually in the form of scores and grades. Assessments provides a general picture—a snapshot—of what students know and are able to do.

Many Serious Difficulties

Evaluation procedures may include multiple-choice, true/false, and short-answer tests that attempt to provide data about how well students retain information. Each measure always includes a value judgment of the student's recall knowledge. This usually takes the form of a statistic, a grade, or an evaluative statement, such as "Bill got a B in science," "Ninety percent of the students got the correct answer," or "This is a poorly written paper."

Evaluation procedures are the most common methods of assessment because they use tests that are simple to administer, score, and grade. But there are several serious dif-

ficulties with evaluation procedures.

One difficulty is that evaluation formats tend to measure the recall of facts and not the broader goals of student understanding and use of science concepts and process skills as described in the Standards. Evaluation testing formats do not allow for the expression of creativity or the development of original solutions to problems.

Another difficulty is that at the district or state level, tests often shape and limit what is taught and learned because textbooks and teachers structure student experiences to meet the content of the tests. In other words they "teach to the test."

Yet another difficulty is that these procedures foster false competitiveness and value comparisons. Students are often rank-ordered by their scores. They are challenged to get high scores or grades rather than being challenged to learn to think, to solve a problem, or to understand a concept. Such procedures are especially damaging when they are used by school systems to evaluate schools or teachers.

Finally, the data derived from evaluation procedures gives no information about how the result was achieved or what to do next. In the examples above, you don't know why "Bill got a B."; therefore, you cannot give him suggestions on how to improve his work. You cannot tell why 10 percent of the students did not get the "right" answer (and there always is one right answer in evaluation), so you cannot help them. You do not know what was "poorly written" about the report so that, if it were yours, you could learn from the experience.

How Assessment Is Different

Assessment plans, as described in the Science Standards, use a variety of formats to derive information about what students understand, what they are able to do, and how they can use their new information/knowledge. These plans have two very important positive features.

First, they are more descriptive than judgmental:
- Bill is able to design and carry out experiments, but he has difficulty figuring out what the results mean.
- When asked to set up a demonstration and explain how a lever works, nine out of ten students showed they understood the concept. One showed partial understanding.
- The content of the report is disorganized so that it is hard for the reader to know what the main topic is and where you are going with it.

Note that in each of the above examples, enough information is provided so that both the teacher and the learner know what needs to be done to improve the work.

Second, assessment plans take into account that there is more to learning about how well students perform than whether an answer is correct.

Assessment of *understanding* is what is critical—for example, the ability to explain why certain steps were taken in trying to answer a question.

To become scientifically literate, students need to be able to use process skills, understand science concepts, and be able to apply their knowledge to finding answers and solving problems. Paper-and-pencil tests have a limited role, but assessments that involve oral and written explanations, modeling, and problem solving (using what has been learned for a purpose) truly assess learning.

Assessing Students

The five Assessment Standards, all of which apply to the elementary grades, address these issues:
- Designing an assessment is a difficult task; the result-

ing data drives the curriculum and influences decisions about students. Every assessment tool should be crafted so that educators can measure clearly stated outcomes accurately.

- As teachers measure student achievement, they must always compare their results to the standard of

"opportunity to learn." Test scores reflect what students know, and also teachers' knowledge and skills, the degree of coordination in the program, the equipment and environment available for student experiences, and the community support behind student growth.

- Assessment data fuels decisions about students, teachers, programs, and systems. There must be confidence in the technical quality of that data. Assessments must be valid, authentic, and reliable. Decisionmakers must have data in which the confidence level is consistent with the consequence of the

decision to be made.

- In assessment, as in teaching, care must always be taken to avoid stereotypes and bias. Just as the styles of learners differ, their perspectives may vary based on their background, environment, or areas of ability. Assessment practices must accommodate diversity, and assessment data must always be examined for signs of bias.
- Assessments influence the plans teachers make for students, courses, and programs. As teachers move toward the Standards, they will rely on data each step of the way. It is crucial that in each decision, teachers keep in mind the strengths, weaknesses, assumptions, and inaccuracies inherent in every assessment.

Using the above guidelines, the Standards suggest a range of ways to assess students: projects that may take hours or days to complete; tasks that involve students in

applying knowledge; and portfolios that house sets of examples that show progress, thinking, and learning.

It is important for teachers to become familiar with and skilled in creating and using these nontraditional formats. Once teachers begin using well-designed curricula and encourage inquiry, and once students become thinkers and problem solvers, then traditional tests will be inadequate for determining what students know and can do. If teachers and curricula change, then the method we use to test and what we test must also change.

Share the Message

The messages in the Assessment Standards are straightforward:

- Good teachers assess their students continually, not just at test time. This helps teachers pace instruction.
- Assessments gauge the opportunities students have for learning, as well as their abilities to take advantage of these opportunities. It is very important to look at *every* set of test data for what it tells us about learners, and what it tells us about the *opportunities* we have provided *for* the learners. In states where comparisons of test scores between districts make front-page headlines, it is common to find that some districts with lower scores also have lower-quality facilities and lower per-capita support for education.
- New types of assessments

take time and may look very different from the ones with which students and parents are familiar.

- Assessments must be fair and unbiased. Like teaching, assessment must accommodate the individual differences of each student.
- The information from any one assessment is only one piece of the puzzle that makes up instruction.

Choosing Assessments

Elementary teachers have a variety of new, or alternative, types of assessment from which to choose. Many teachers will opt to combine different methods when evaluating different aspects of individual student progress. Here are three assessment examples:

Performance based assessment involves giving one or more students a task that will enable the teacher to see a conclusion from the student(s), and the process used to find that answer. Frequently these types of assessment have no one correct answer, and they model the kind of activities that usually take place during science instruction.

Portfolios are generally examples of individual student work that indicate progress, improvement, accomplishment, or special challenges. Teachers collect and assess the work of their students throughout the school year.

Open-ended questions mimic good classroom strategies and encourage thinking. These questions are particularly helpful to teachers in understanding how students go about finding an answer, solving a problem, or drawing a conclusion.

Science journal writing captures a dimension of students' conceptual understanding that is different from that which is usually measured by other types of assessment. Children are able to record procedures and results from investigations as well as observations, hypotheses, and inferences about science phenomena.

Perhaps the greatest gain for teachers in using challenging and exciting alternative assessment methods is the difference they can see in the development of meaningful modes of inquiry by their students.

The pathway to better assessment may be a new one for some teachers, but there is a wealth of information in the list of resources below that elementary teachers can tap to help them get started.

LISA CROOKS

Association for Supervision and Curriculum Development (ASCD). (1995). *Designing Performance Assessment Tasks.* Alexandria, VA: Author.

Barrow, Lloyd H. (1993, November/December). A Portfolio of Learning. *Science and Children, 31* (3), 38–39.

Bergman, Abby Bary. (1993, February). Performance Assessment for Early Childhood. *Science and Children, 30* (5), 20–22.

Bonnstetter, Ronald J. (1992, March). Where Can Teachers Go for More Information on Portfolios? *Science Scope, 15* (6), 28.

Collins, Angelo. (1992, March.) Portfolios: Questions for Design. *Science Scope, 15* (6), 25–27.

Doran, Rodney L., and **Hejaily, Nicholas.** (1992, March). Hands-on Evaluation: A How-To Guide. *Science Scope, 15* (6), 9–11.

Doran, Rodney, Chan, Fred, and Tamir, Pinchas. (1998). *Science Educators* Guide to Assessment. Arlington, VA: National Science Teachers Association.

Finson, Kevin D., and **Beaver, John B.** (1994, September). Performance Assessment: Getting Started. *Science Scope, 18* (1), 44–49.

Foster, Gerald William, and **Heiting, William Anton.** (1994, October). Embedded Assessment. *Science and Children, 32* (2), 30–33.

Hardy, Garry R., Sudweeks, Richard R., Tolman, Marvin N., Tolman, Richard R., and **Baird, J. Hugh.** (1991, October). Does Listening Ability Affect Test Scores? *Science and Children, 29* (2), 43–45.

Hart, Diane. (1994). *Authentic Assessment: A Handbook for Educators.* Menlo Park, CA: Addison-Wesley.

Hein, George E. (Ed.). (1990). *The Assessment of Hands-On Elementary Science Programs.* Fargo, ND: Center for Teaching and Learning, University of North Dakota.

Hein, George E., and **Price, Sabra.** (1994). *Active Assessment for Science: A Guide for Elementary School Teachers.* Portsmouth, NJ: Heinemann.

Herman, Joan L., Aschbacher, Pamela R., and **Winters, Lynn.** (1992). *A Practical Guide to Alternative Assessment.* Alexandria, VA: Association for Supervision and Curriculum Development (ASCD).

Jones, M. Gail. (1994, October). Assessment Potpourri. *Science and Children, 32* (2), 14–17.

Kenney, Evelyn, and **Perry, Suzanne.** (1994, October). Talking with Parents About Performance-Based Report Cards. *Educational Leadership, 52* (2), 24–27.

Kleinheider, Janet K. (1996, January). Assessment Matters. *Science and Children, 33* (4), 23–25, 41.

Liftig, Inez Fugate, Liftig, Bob, and **Eaker, Karen.** (1992, March). Making Assessment Work: What Teachers Should Know Before They Try It. *Science Scope, 15* (6), 4, 6, 8.

Luft, Julie. (1997, February). Design Your Own Rubric. *Science Scope, 20* (5), 25–27.

McMahon, Maureen M., and **Yocum, Charles.** (1994, October). Video Quizzes: An Alternative Assessment. *Science and Children, 32* (2), 18–20.

Meng, Elizabeth, and **Doran, Rodney L.** (1990, September). What Research Says...About Appropriate Methods of Assessment. *Science and Children, 28* (1), 42–45.

Moran, Jeffrey B., and **Boulter, William.** (1992, March). Step-by-Step Scoring. *Science Scope, 15* (6), 46–47, 59.

Nott, Linda, Reeve, Colleen, and **Reeve, Raymond.** (1992, March). Scoring Rubrics: An Assessment Option. *Science Scope, 15* (6), 44–45.

O'Neil, J. Peter. (1994, January). Portfolio Pointers. *Science Scope, 17* (4), 32.

Price, Sabra, and **Hein, George E.** (1994, October). Scoring Active Assessments. *Science and Children, 32* (2), 26–29.

Reichel, Anne Grall. (1994, October). Performance Assessment: Five Practical Approaches. *Science and Children, 32* (2), 21–25.

Roth, Wolff-Michael. (1992, March). Dynamic Evaluation. *Science Scope, 15* (6), 37–40.

Shepardson, Daniel P., and **Britsch, Susan J.** (1997, February). Children's Science Journals: Tools for Teaching, Learning, and Assessing. *Science and Children, 34* (5), 13–17, 46–47.

Smith, Paul G. (1995, September). Reveling in Rubrics. *Science Scope, 19* (1), 34–36.

Tetenbaum, Zelda. (1992, March). An Ordered Approach. *Science Scope, 15* (6), 12, 14, 18.

Tippins, Deborah J., and **Dana, Nancy Fichtman.** (1992, March). Culturally Relevant Alternative Assessment. *Science Scope, 15* (6), 50–53.

Tolman, Marvin N., Baird, J. Hugh, and **Hardy, Gary R.** (1994, October). Let the Tool Fit the Task. *Science and Children, 32* (2), 18–20.

Tolman, Marvin N., Sudweeks, Richard, Baird, J. Hugh, and **Tolman, Richard R.** (1991, September). Does Reading Ability Affect Science Test Scores? *Science and Children, 29* (1), 44–47.

U.S. Department of Education, Office of Educational Research and Improvement. (1993, November). *Student Portfolios: Administrative Uses.* Consumer Guide No. 8. Washington, DC: Author.

U.S. Department of Education, Office of Educational Research and Improvement. (1993, December). *Student Portfolios: Classroom Uses.* Consumer Guide No. 9. Washington, DC: Author.

Wise, Kevin C. (1993, September). New Teacher Feature: Testing Tips. *Science Scope, 17* (1), 51–52.

The full text to most of these resources is available on NSTA's supplementary *Resources for the Road* CD-ROM.

Changing Emphases

The National Science Education Standards envision change throughout the system. The Assessment Standards encompass the following changes in emphases:

LESS EMPHASIS ON	MORE EMPHASIS ON
Assessing what is easily measured	Assessing what is most highly valued
Assessing discrete knowledge	Assessing rich, well-structured knowledge
Assessing scientific knowledge	Assessing scientific understanding and reasoning
Assessing to learn what students do not know	Assessing to learn what students do understand
Assessing only achievement	Assessing achievement and opportunity to learn
End-of-term assessment by teachers	Students engaged in ongoing assessment of their work and that of others
Development of external assessments by measurement experts alone	Teachers involved in the development of external assessments

Content Standards

Science is a process of discovery

Mapping the Content Standards

PATTY NEW

The Content Standards offer us much more than just a traditional listing of content objectives. The Standards recognize that children change over time and that effective teaching must respect and parallel these changes in a consistent way. The Standards shift the emphasis from presenting scientific knowledge through lecture and demonstration to encouraging active learning where students learn with understanding.

The Standards emphasize that, for students, the essence of learning science lies not in memorizing facts, but in carrying out the processes of inquiry—asking questions, making observations, and gathering, organizing, and analyzing data.

The eight categories of the Content Standards describe what all students should "know, understand and be able to do" as a result of experiencing science in the classroom. Together, the Content Standards define the breadth of the science content to be taught; but they do not provide the organization for a sci-

ence curriculum. Organization is left to us as teachers and to schools, curriculum designers, and communities.

An effective curriculum provides emphasis, balance, integration of content, and detail and additional content when needed.

Content Standards describe goals for student understanding, not the instructional experiences through which our students will develop that understanding. That is for the teachers and the school administer to develop.

Standards Applicable to the Elementary Grades

The first category of the Content Standards, Unifying Concepts and Processes, applies to grades K-12. The National Research Council presents the other seven categories Standards A through G in clusters for grades K-4, 5-8, and 9-12. (For a list of all the National Science Education Standards, see Appendix B.)

In this section, you will find examples of how some of the topics in the Standards might be taught in elementary school. We have applied these examples to smaller grade ranges than those used by the National Research Council: primary elementary (grades K-2), middle elementary (grades 3-4), and upper elementary (grades 5-6). These ranges are not prescriptive, but are meant to suggest how the Content Standards might be applied in a K-6 curriculum.

Because it was not possible within the constraints of this book to cover every topic at every grade, we have selected topics from each Standard, including at least one for each grade range (primary, middle, and upper elementary). In some cases a single Standard is illustrated for all three levels; in others, the Standards for grades K-4 and 5-8 are not the same, and we illustrate the different Standards.

Each selected topic is described within the context of the Teaching and Assessment Standards—each has relevant information about the learner and comments about instructional and assessment possibilities. A classroom vignette follows each selected topic. These examples are illustrations, they do not attempt to "cover" the topics in depth.

In each content category you will find a list of Programs, Resources for the Road, and Internet links that exemplify teaching consistent with the spirit of the Standards. Many of these resources, including all those from *Science and Children* and *Science Scope*, are available on NSTA's supplementary *Resources of the Road CD-ROM*.

Unifying Concepts and Processes

The K-12 Unifying Concepts and Processes Standard, which highlights the connections between scientific ideas, is not specifically addressed in this book. While that Standard can be the focus of instruction at any grade level, it is generally taught in the context of the other Content Standards. For example, the meaning of measurement and how to use measurement tools are a natural part of any investigation. These ideas are introduced frequently throughout the early grades. Understanding the unifying principles of change, constancy, and measurement will help older students develop a "big picture" of scientific ideas—in this case, how measurement is important in all scientific endeavors.

The Unifying Concepts and Processes are
- Systems, order, and organization
- Evidence, models, and explanation
- Constancy, change, and measurement
- Evolution and equilibrium
- Form and function

Although these are sophisticated concepts, we can introduce them in developmentally appropriate ways in the elementary grades. We might ask students to reflect on these ideas in relation to the content being learned. Then, as students build a repertoire of experience over the years, they can extend their reflection across the disciplines.

Only after much experience in different settings will students develop a fuller understanding of these fundamental and powerful ideas that characterize science.

Nature
of
the
Learner

KELLY A. HUFF BENKOSKI

PATRICIA RAMEY

KATE McGRATH

Most primary level students have a natural interest in almost everything around them. They explore the world using all of their senses. They push, pull, and transform objects by acting upon them. They explore their world by watching what others do, mimicking them exactly. These children often make inquiries by guessing about how things work and behave. They tend to believe whatever adults tell them.

Young children's natural capacities for inquiry can be seen when they observe, sort, group, and order objects. Sometimes they do this consciously, and sometimes without any plan at all. Even without being taught, primary level children pair objects in one-to-one correspondences. Pairings are made on the basis of single attributes inherent in objects (e.g. shape, color, and size). The objects may be arranged in various ways—side by side, in piles, or in a chained linear sequence. By pairing, children learn basic concepts about how things are alike or different.

Primary students have difficulty classifying objects using several characteristics. But with their ability to do one-to-one correspondences, they can solve some very complex problems if allowed to work through them, step by step, through trial and error. Adults who become anxious over a child's error tend either to "help" the child by showing how an adult would perform the task, or reprimand the child for the mistake. Neither of these actions serves the child well. Children learn from their errors and must be given the chance to work through them.

Primary level children are somewhat egocentric and believe that everyone sees the world the way they do, so they tend to talk at rather than with people. In spite of being egocentric, they can learn to take turns and ensure that social interactions are fair. Primary level children may have difficulty working with others or appreciating other people's point of view.

The K-2 students easily understand and remember stories that unfold in a linear way. Stories about seasons, the water cycle, life cycles, and so on can be effective teaching tools. Remembering a story may not be the equivalent of understanding the story. Primary students learn best by building understanding from their own actions upon objects and by telling stories about what they did and what they found out.

As they impose their ideas on the world, trying things out to see what will happen (poking, pushing, feeling, etc.), children see the results of their actions and thus come to understand how part of their world works. If these experiences are connected with language experiences (e.g., talking with students as they explore instead of having a summary discussion after an exploration) primary students will learn how to express what they have learned in clear and accurate terms.

PRESIDENTIAL AWARDS

Middle elementary grade students retain the learning capabilities that they developed at the primary level and begin to experience a broad view of the world.

The mental construct of the middle grade student is comprehensive, and has a rationale or a logic to it. Instead of being satisfied with matching objects, they tend to want to create large, complex organizations. If a student puts leaves together on the basis of their shapes, then a logical arrangement has been made by imposing a singular rule on the objects. Students are able to discover and understand singular rules if they are given the opportunity.

Students are now able to communicate in various ways. In addition to their speaking skills, they are able to take simple notes, record data, and keep simple journals. They are less egocentric than in previous years, and are capable of working well in pairs and, occasionally, in large groups. Friendships develop through the sharing of common views.

They are now able to think back through a story to find the cause of an event. Because they understand antecedents, they begin to make simple predictions about outcomes. They no longer see concepts such as life cycles and the water cycle as

GARRISON HALL

linear sequences of events (e.g., egg, larva, pupae, butterfly) but rather as a continuous, repeatable chain of sequences that has no beginning and no end.

Even their stories are no longer confined to linear concepts. If students write: "The boy ran" and add "to the shore", and then add "to collect sea shells", they can return to the original sentence by taking away the prepositional phrases. In fact, given opportunity and practice, students are able to transpose the component parts of a linear sequence and understand that the variations do not alter the original concept (e.g., "to collect sea shells, the boy ran to the shore").

As inquirers, middle school students are able to design simple, comparative tests (not experiments). They carry out the tests, analyze results, and communicate their findings to others. They might wonder if the fingerprint pattern on their right hand is the same as on their left. When asked how they would find out, they will say "Check the fingerprints on the left hand" (a simple comparative test). They will be able to interpret the results and give a reasonable answer to their original question. As long as they have the necessary resources, students are capable of designing many kinds of simple tests, and gather and interpret information to answer their own questions.

Students entering upper elementary levels continue to be good observers, and retain all the abilities developed in previous years. They now learn about cause and effect and how to record data describing those relationships.

These students can be guided from trial-and-error thinking (following a "recipe") to comparing two or more situations in which events occur simultaneously, but under different conditions. Their ability to inquire becomes more "experimental" and is much more advanced than simple comparative tests. They generate simple hypotheses, conduct tests, record and analyze data to find evidence for supporting or not supporting the original hypothesis. They can determine whether or not a test is "fair". They have difficulty identifying *all* the variables that influence an experiment and they are not able to infer the importance of a finding to a broader purpose than the task at hand.

Students at the upper elementary level are much less egocentric than in previous years. They are interested in what other people do and in events that are remote from their surroundings. They work well in collaborative groups. They appreciate different points of view and build evidence to support a point of view. They recognize that more than one point of view might be valid at the same time and will not be upset by such an ambiguity. As they move through this level, they begin to imagine events from perspectives other than their own.

The writing skills of upper grade students allow them to keep extensive journals, diaries, records of information over time, and to prepare written reports based on these records. They are able to generate and interpret graphs and understand that a point on a graph is influenced by two variables at the same time. They understand complex storylines where more than one idea is being discussed simultaneously. They interpolate and extrapolate from linear stories. They reason through simple statements of logic to determine whether or not they are true (e.g. some multiples of 3 are odd (true); some odd numbers are multiples of 3 (true); all odd numbers are multiples of 3 (false)).

At the upper elementary level teaching science content can be greatly expanded. However, this should involve content that has value and gives opportunities for the students to use their current thinking skills. If the content is carefully selected and embedded within an inquiry-oriented curriculum, students will begin to recognize the commonalties in the content of the various branches of science.

NANCY MARRA

Approximate Conversions from Metric Measures

Symbol	When you know	Multiply by	To Find	Symbol
LENGTH				
mm	millimeters	0.04	inches	in
cm	centimeters	0.4	inches	in
m	meters	3.3	feet	ft
m	meters	1.1	yards	yd
km	kilometers	0.6	miles	mi
AREA				
cm^2	square centimeters	0.16	square inches	in^2
m^2	square meters	1.2	square yards	yd^2
km^2	square kilometers	0.4	square miles	mi^2
hm^2	hectares (10,000 m^2)	2.5	acres	
MASS				
g	grams	0.035	ounces	oz
kg	kilograms	2.2	pounds	lb
t	metric ton (1,000 kg)	1.1	short tons	
VOLUME				
mL	milliliters	0.03	fluid ounces	fl oz
mL	milliliters	0.06	cubic inches	in^3
L	liters	2.1	pints	pt
L	liters	1.06	quarts	qt
L	liters	0.26	gallons	gal
m^3	cubic meters	35.	cubic feet	ft^3
m^3	cubic meters	1.3	cubic yards	yd^3
TEMPERATURE (exact)				
°C	degrees Celsius	multiply by 9/5 then add 32	degrees Fahrenheit	°F

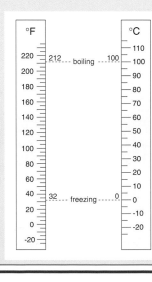

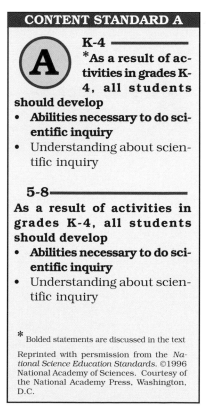

Scientific knowledge is constantly changing. As more research is conducted and as advanced technology enhances our ability to make observations, our knowledge of the world changes. Knowing that science is a continuous process of inquiry helps students understand its dynamic nature and recognize that in science change is the rule rather than the exception.

When we teach science as inquiry we need to shift from a dependence on textbooks as the basic source of information to using texts and books as **references**. Hands-on activities are central when students investigate the world through inquiry. Often, students discover facts, concepts, and laws of science in much the same way that the original discoverers did. The Standards' emphasis on firsthand observations in learning science concepts reflects the belief that students learn best by being directly involved in their own learning.

This view of learning emphasizes the logical thinking processes by which new knowledge is acquired and de-emphasizes learning by rote. With the speed at which scientific knowledge is expanding, it is becoming more difficult to prescribe which facts and concepts should be presented to elementary students. So it makes more sense to teach them the **processes** of science—inquiry skills that enable them to construct their own knowledge. These abilities serve students well by giving them the tools with which they can acquire additional knowledge in the future.

Perhaps because knowing how to conduct scientific inquiry is considered so important, the pathway to this Standard specifies the abilities needed for each level and provides some explanation for each.

To develop scientific inquiry skills, K-4 students should be able to
- plan and conduct a simple investigation
- employ simple equipment and tools to gather data
- use data to construct reasonable explanations
- communicate the results of the investigations and give explanations

For levels 5-8, students should be able to
- ask questions that can be answered by scientific investigations
- design and conduct a scientific investigation
- use appropriate tools and techniques to gather, analyze, and interpret data
- develop descriptions, explanations, predictions, and models based on evidence
- think critically and logically to discover the relationship between evidence and explanation

Science is a process of discovery. Teaching science as inquiry requires a learning environment in which students engage in hands-on activities and investigations so that they can explore the world and discover its patterns.

CONTENT STANDARD A

A

K-4
*****As a result of activities in grades K-4, all students should develop**
- **Abilities necessary to do scientific inquiry**
- Understanding about scientific inquiry

5-8
As a result of activities in grades K-4, all students should develop
- **Abilities necessary to do scientific inquiry**
- Understanding about scientific inquiry

***** Bolded statements are discussed in the text

Nature of the Learner

We see the natural inquiry capacities of young children as they observe objects and sort, group, and order them. By using these abilities and by talking about what they are doing, young children learn a great deal about the world.

Get Ready for Science

The most important tool that children at the primary level use is observation. Curiosity makes students eager to explore by working with objects and asking questions. They learn about objects by grouping and ordering them. Such exploration provides early experiences in organizing data and understanding processes.

Get Set for Instruction

Because young children need to work individually to construct their own knowledge, it is important that we provide a variety of objects, in sets, for free exploration, with each child having his or her own set. In addition to structured time, we need to allow time for play.

We should offer a variety of activities that let children use all their senses, allowing them to explore at their own pace and to self-regulate their experiences. We should encourage them to interact with others, share their thoughts, and learn from the feedback they hear from one another. Our questions will stimulate children's curiosity, help them understand what they are learning, and require more than a "yes" or "no" answer.

Assessment

Our questions and observations should focus on the many ways that children group objects. Students almost always have a reason for the grouping, but many are unable to express it.

Watch students as they put a variety of objects in order. Are the groups based on a common attribute? Do they use objects to create pictures rather than form groups? Do they arrange objects in rows, in patterns, or in haphazard ways? As we watch what children do and have them explain their groups, we uncover clues to their understanding.

When plants are discussed, we might use an activity in sorting leaves to assess how well students recognize leaf attributes (shape, edges, tips, etc.) and use these characteristics to categorize the leaves. When studying seashells or rocks and minerals, students can do the same kinds of activities and be assessed on them.

In general, we will want to know how well inquiry is leading students to learning scientific concepts. For example, after examining leaves, can the students describe the characteristics of the leaves in detail? Can they explain how some leaves are similar to each other and others are different? Can they tell you how they chose the characteristics, and can they describe these characteristics?

Primary Elementary, grades K-2

Go! An Example of a Classroom in Action

Gloria Chin's classroom has a variety of objects in sets that can be grouped or sorted. These have a number of characteristics, such as color, shape, size, texture, diameter, and length. Students sort the objects into groups based on some of these characteristics or put them in order according to size or length. There are enough sets so that each student is able to work alone.

The beginning sets of materials include keys, buttons, feathers, pasta of different shapes, paint sample strips, nuts and bolts, and beans. Advanced sets of materials (leaves, seeds, shells, nuts, rocks, dowels of different diameters, and dowels of different lengths) expose students to content related to the sciences, such as leaf characteristics.

While the students are sorting their objects, Ms. Chin observes them and asks about the ways they are making the groupings. She understands that, at this level, the ability to communicate ideas is critical. Many of her students are at the early stage of understanding classification and will group objects mainly by a single characteristics or will arrange the pieces to make a house, a group of people, or some symbolic representation.

Ms. Chin moves around the room and watches and listens to individual children as they make decisions. She keeps anecdotal notes on each child. You might hear her ask such questions as:
• Can you put the ones that go together into piles?
• Tell me how you decided where to put this piece.

Primary Elementary, grades K-2

SCIENCE AS INQUIRY

CONTENT STANDARD A   K-4

Abilities necessary to do scientific inquiry

Nature of the Learner

At the middle elementary level, students are able to master some of the skills of a good inquirer. For example, most students can make measurements using different tools—rulers, clocks, thermometers, containers, and balances.

Preparing for Science

In general, inquiry involves posing a question, making observations, clarifying the task, planning an investigation, deciding what data should be collected, gathering that data, reflecting on whether additional data is needed, analyzing the data to construct reasonable explanations, and communicating results. Influencing these processes are personal attitudes, experiences, and emotions. Inquiry is a driving force in advancing scientific knowledge.

The most useful tools that the scientist has include: an attitude of openness, the ability to make observations, taking careful measurements, and recording observations and measurements. Scientists use different kinds of investigations depending on the questions they are trying to answer. They vary their thinking processes and strategies to fit the task at hand.

Nature of Instruction

Students become better inquirers when we give them opportunities to generate their own questions and to design ways to find answers to these questions.

Often, open-ended inquiry will follow from a starting activity that captures students' interest. For example, if we show students how they can capture a print of the finger pattern on their right thumb (by rubbing their thumb across a patch of pencil scribbles, placing the sticky side of a strip of transparent tape against the dirtied thumb, then taping the strip to a sheet of paper), they might ask, "Do all my fingers have the same pattern?" "Will the thumb on my other hand be the same?" "Do my toes have prints?" "Are my prints like my parents' prints?" With so many questions to choose from, it's time to let students find answers to their questions.

Sometimes an opportunity for inquiry occurs unexpectedly in the classroom. We should capitalize on these moments by helping students' search for information.

Assessment

There are several ways to assess student skills in asking questions and planning investigations. We might ask them to analyze the plans: What is the question? Is the plan organized? Are we testing only one variable at a time? Will measurements be needed?

While the students carry out their plans, we can use other questions to guide assessment: How well do the students record data? How do they interpret the data? We observe and question students as they work, or we read their journals.

For example, we could ask students to determine which kind of cloth creates the most static electricity when rubbed on a balloon. We would note whether students test one material at a time. Do they use the same number of rubs for each test? How do they test for the "most" static electricity? Is it determined by the number of small pieces of paper that adhere to the balloon, how long the balloon sticks to a wall, or some other criterion? Do students repeat a test several times to determine if the same thing will happen more than once? We jot down the answers to these and other questions on note cards for later reference.

SUZANNE HENDERSON

Middle Elementary, Grades 3-4

SCIENCE AS INQUIRY

CONTENT STANDARD A   K-4

Abilities necessary to do scientific inquiry

An Example of a Classroom in Action

PRESIDENTIAL AWARDS

Mary Stewart introduces some simple chemistry concepts by giving her students unknown materials to compare and contrast for similarities and differences. She prepares five numbered envelopes for each group of four students in which she places 25 mL (5 teaspoons) of each of the following materials:

- *Envelope 1:* granular dextrose or glucose from a local drugstore
- *Envelope 2:* powdered starch from the grocery store
- *Envelope 3:* baking soda
- *Envelope 4:* an equal mixture of dextrose (or glucose) and starch
- *Envelope 5:* an equal mixture of dextrose (or glucose) and baking soda

After giving each group a set of the first three envelopes, she has them place 5 mL (1 tsp) from each of these envelopes on separate places on a piece of wax paper. Students examine the white substances using all their senses *except* taste (Ms. Stewart has already explained that it is dangerous to taste unfamiliar substances). Students record their observations in a table and discuss the limitations of their senses in identifying the materials. When the students finish, Ms. Stewart tells them the names of the materials.

Ms. Stewart demonstrates how to conduct indicator tests that will show the presence of the known materials. The tests used indicators such as

- water. Do some of the materials dissolve and others not?
- iodine—indicates the presence of starch by turning a blue-black color. Does the color of some materials change when iodine is added?
- vinegar—indicates the presence of a carbonate by "fizzing". Do some materials react to vinegar?
- Benedict's solution—indicates the presence of simple sugars by changing the material to a red-copper color. Do some materials react to the solution?

On another day, Ms. Stewart gives her students envelopes 4 and 5 and describes their contents as mystery mixtures, each containing a mixture of two of the already identified materials. She invites students to find what two substances make up each mixture. By applying their knowledge from the earlier observations and tests to the mystery mixtures, students discover what each mixture has in it.

SAFETY NOTES:
- *Always have children wear goggles if they are using chemicals that can splash.*
- *Some elementary classrooms do not allow the use of iodine. Iodine is poisonous, and its stains are difficult to remove. Wash hands after use.*

Primary Elementary, Grades 3-4

Nature of the Learner

At the upper elementary level, most students observe phenomena accurately. They begin to create and interpret coordinate graphs and understand models that explain inferential ideas.

Preparing for Science

Science is inquiry at work, an unending quest for knowledge about the universe and all the objects in it. Reliance on established procedures of inquiry to find the truest explanations of observed events is one of the distinctive characteristics of science.

Controlling Variables. One of the most important inquiry procedures is experimentation. For example, we have a cart which rolls down an incline plane to flat land. If we wonder which parts of the cart affect the distance it travels, we make a list of possible factors (variables) like the weight of the cart, the shape of the cart, the size of the wheels, etc. Then we test the variables one at a time, keeping the other variables the same, to determine which variables affect the movement of the cart.

Coordinate Graphing. Graphing is an important way in which inquirers organize certain types of data. Whenever there is a relationship between two variables, a coordinate graph can be used. Use whole or rational numbers for the coordinates depending on the students' experience with two-dimensional graphs.

Data must be collected for two variables for each trial, even though only one variable is being tested. For example,

if the slope of the inclined plane, the nature of the plane's surface, the release system, and other factors are held constant, and a cart of known weight is released, the distance the cart travels can be measured. To test a variable, in this case the weight of the cart, hold everything else constant, changing only the weight of the cart for each trial. The distance the cart travels can be recorded for several trials. The data, weight and distance, are then used to create a coordinate graph. The graph's pattern will tell something about the variable's effect on the distance the cart traveled.

Nature of Instruction

Because students of this age are less egocentric than in earlier grades, they are capable of working well in collaborative groups in which students take responsibility for solving problems. Because cooperation requires distinctive roles and responsibilities, it is important that all students have opportunities to experience *each* role. In collaborative groupings, each member contributes his or her talents to the activity of the group. Although roles may be assigned, the roles are of secondary importance to the collaboration. Of course, there will also be times when students will want to pursue an inquiry on their own.

Assessment

Students are able to grasp some of the most important scientific concepts, inquiring into the cause-and-effect relationships between objects and events. Determining relationships requires a different thinking process than categorizing objects based on their characteristics.

One way we assess students' ability to inquire in this way is to explore their understanding of relationships as they design and carry out controlled experiments.

Upper Elementary, grades 5-6

SUZANNE MALY

An Example of a Classroom in Action

Jose Fernandez is inviting his class to design and build a cart that rolls down a ramp freely.

He asks his students what components a cart has that enables it to move. They respond that carts need wheels in order to move. They discuss whether the number, size, and position of the wheels makes a difference. Then they plan the building of their carts.

When the carts are built, the students test them by rolling them down a ramp. They talk about some common features of the carts, such as wheels that are fixed so that they and the axle turn as a unit, or the use of bearings that allow the wheels to turn by themselves.

The students start to think about what they could do to their carts to make them suitable for transportation. They decide to make self-propelled carts.

Mr. Fernandez challenges them to modify their carts to travel 2 meters on level ground without an external push or pull. He asks for suggestions, which he lists on the chalkboard. Then he demonstrates how to wind a rubber band around an axle so as to drive the wheels, suggesting that students use different-sized rubber bands.

How to attach the rubber band

Cut the rubber band and tie one end to the axle and the other end to a stationary part of the cart—the "chassis". Holding the cart in your hand, roll the axle so that the rubber band is wound tightly around it. Put the cart down, the rubber band will unroll, and the axle will turn.

Students discover that when the axle makes a turn, the wheels go around once. Mr. Fernandez asks how far a cart would go if the wheels rotated just once. The students respond that the distance will be equal to the circumference of the wheel.

Then Mr. Fernandez suggests that the students make their carts go farther, but without winding the rubber bands any tighter. The students discover that larger wheels cover more distance with each rotation.

The students try to make their carts travel at least 2 meters. They draw a graph that shows the distance that wheels of different diameters carry a cart when the rubber band is wound 10 times around the axle. They use the graph to predict the wheel size that is needed to go exactly 2 meters on 10 winds.

PROGRAMS FOR ELEMENTARY SCIENCE

PRIMARY ELEMENTARY - GRADES K-2

Full Options Science System (FOSS)
Each module allows students to explore through trial-and-error, observing, comparing, and organizing.

Insights (EDC)
The Senses Module
Children are encouraged to use all their senses to observe and describe objects and phenomena.

Science for Life and Living (BSCS)
Comparison and Evidence Unit
Students use direct observations as evidence for their decisions or conclusions about change.

MIDDLE ELEMENTARY - GRADES 3-4

Full Option Science System (FOSS)
Measurement Module
Students use metric tools to make measurements: linear (rulers), volume (containers), temperature (thermometers), weight (mass) (balance). Students are taught to *think* metrically in making estimates and measurements.

Full Option Science System (FOSS)
Ideas and Inventions Module
Students use unusual tools for discovering patterns (e.g., chromatography, rubbings, and mirror images).

Great Explorations in Math and Science (GEMS)
Crime Lab Chemistry Unit
Students use paper chromatography to see which of several pens was used to write a ransom note.

Great Explorations in Math and Science (GEMS)
Fingerprinting Unit
Students take their own fingerprints and use a classification system to solve a crime.

Science and Technology for Children (STC)
Comparing and Measuring Unit
Students use linear measurements to make comparisons between objects.

Science for Life and Living (BSCS)
Records and Data Unit
Students keep detailed records to improve their observational and organizational skills.

UPPER ELEMENTARY - GRADES 5-6

Full Option Science System (FOSS)
Variables Module
Students manage variab]les to determine cause-and-effect relationships. Includes development of graphing skills.

Great Explorations in Math and Science (GEMS)
Paper Towel Testing Unit
Students experiment to rank wet strength and absorbency of four brands of paper towels.

Science and Technology for Children (STC)
Measuring Time Unit
Students measure time by the movement of the Sun, and changes in phases of the moon, and they construct a mechanical clock.

Science for Life and Living (BSCS)
Interactions and Variables Unit
Students learn about variables, and design experiments to help them answer questions.

See appendix D for addresses

RESOURCES FOR THE ROAD

Baird, Hugh. (1994, November/December). Keying out Banana Splits. *Science Scope. 18* (3), 12-16.

Barry, Dana Malloy. (1990, September). Fat Burgers. *Science Scope. 14* (1), 34-36.

Henney, and Woods. (1991, September). The Key to Connected Learning. *Communicator, XXI,* pp. 28-29.

Martin, D. (1991). *Themes in Science: Connections Among Big Ideas.* Sacramento, CA: California Science Teachers Association.

Rakow, Steven J. (1986). *Teaching Science as Inquiry.* Bloomington, IN: Phi Delta Kappa Educational Foundation.

Scarnati, James T. (1993, March). Tracks Revisited. *Science and Children. 30* (6), 23-25.

Spurlin, Quincy. (1995, January). Put Science in a Bag. *Science and Children. 32* (4), 19-22.

Stiles, John R. (1992, November/December). Mealworms: A Year-Round Science Project. *Science Scope. 16* (3), 36-39.

Sumrall, William J., and Criglow, Judy. (1995, March). The "Scoop" on Science Data. *Science and Children. 32* (6), 36-39, 44.

Truho, Gail. (1993, September). Testing Gum, Two, Three .... *Science and Children. 31* (1), 19-21.

The full text to most of these resources is available on NSTA's supplementary *Resources for the Road* CD-ROM.

OTHER TOPICS COVERED BY STANDARD A

Understanding about scientific inquiry, which explains scientific inquiry as practiced by scientists, has not been illustrated. The following Internet link contains information and activities that cover this topic.

Topic: scientific method
Go to: http://www.scilinks.org/
Code: PAE01

Approximate Conversions to Metric Measures

Symbol	When you know	Multiply by	To Find	Symbol
LENGTH				
in	inches	2.5	centimeters	cm
ft	feet	30.	centimeters	cm
yd	yards	0.9	meters	m
mi	miles	1.6	kilometers	km
AREA				
in²	square inches	6.5	square centimeters	cm²
ft²	square feet	0.09	square meters	m²
yd²	square yards	0.8	square meters	m²
mi²	square miles	2.6	square kilometers	km²
	acres	0.4	hectares (10,000 m²)	ha
MASS				
oz	ounces	28.	grams	g
lb	pounds	0.45	kilograms	kg
	short tons (2,000 lb)	0.9	metric ton	t
VOLUME				
tsp	teaspoons	5.	milliliters	mL
Tbsp	tablespoons	15.	milliliters	mL
in³	cubic inches	16.	milliliters	mL
fl oz	fluid ounces	30.	milliliters	mL
c	cups	0.24	liters	L
pt	pints	0.47	liters	L
qt	quarts	0.95	liters	L
gal	gallons	3.8	liters	L
ft³	cubic feet	0.03	cubic meters	m³
yd³	cubic yards	0.76	cubic meters	m³
TEMPERATURE (exact)				
°F	degrees Fahrenheit	subtract 32 mulitply by 5/9	degrees Celsius	°C

PHYSICAL SCIENCE

INTRODUCTION

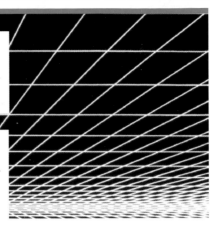

Some of the most effective experiences for learning elementary-level physical science involve the movement or changes in objects and materials. Students learn about objects by observing them and noting similarities and differences, and by acting on them by applying force.

According to Piaget, knowledge about objects develops through learning how they move and change position and shape in relation to the viewer—as when we look at objects from different angles. Experiences with objects moving in space and changing appearance lead children to realize that an object remains the same even when it looks different.

To develop an understanding of the properties of objects and materials, one of the principal topics of the Physical Science Standards, young students need opportunities to alter objects and observe the results of their own actions. Although it may be tempting to emphasize the product rather than the process of change, the changing itself should be the emphasis of the activity.

Activities involving change often require space and are messy. This will call for some creative problem-solving on our part. An activity can be set up so as to minimize messes; space constraints may require reducing the scale of an activity.

The Physical Science Content Standards for the elementary level focus primarily on the properties and motion of objects, and on energy. Students will construct an understanding of these topics by acting on objects and observing what happens to them.

By causing an object to move, students see the direct connection between what they do and how the object changes. Students need to vary their actions to see the possibility of different outcomes. They need to be able to observe the reaction of the object, or they will have no way of seeing the connections between their actions and the effects on the object. Many phenomena in the physical world involve reactions that are not observable, either because of the speed at which the objects move or because the phenomenon is only indirectly observable, as with gravity, magnetism, and electrical force. Finally, the reaction of the object must be immediate. A time lag in reactions makes it difficult for students to see a connection between cause and effect, and misconceptions result.

Thus, concrete experiences and activities involving experimentation are essential for learning the topics in this Standard. However, we should limit the number of variables in these grades, lest the students become confused and misinterpret cause and effect. Using highly visible materials will make it easier for students to observe the movement or changes in objects and derive benefit from the experience.

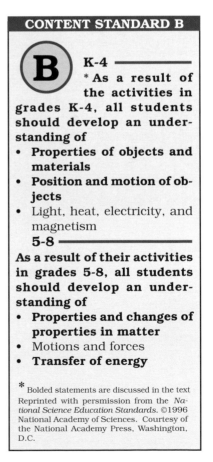

CONTENT STANDARD B

B **K-4**
* As a result of the activities in grades K-4, all students should develop an understanding of

- **Properties of objects and materials**
- **Position and motion of objects**
- Light, heat, electricity, and magnetism

5-8
As a result of their activities in grades 5-8, all students should develop an understanding of

- **Properties and changes of properties in matter**
- Motions and forces
- **Transfer of energy**

* Bolded statements are discussed in the text
Reprinted with persmission from the *National Science Education Standards*. ©1996 National Academy of Sciences. Courtesy of the National Academy Press, Washington, D.C.

Nature of the Learner

At the primary elementary level, most students are able to compare simple objects, communicate their observations and comparisons to others, and increase their vocabulary associated with observations and comparisons.

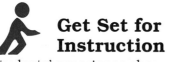

Get Ready for Science

Objects have properties that can be observed, described, measured, and recorded. These include size, weight, shape, color, and temperature. Some properties change over time. Properties of objects, such as hardness or smoothness, describe or characterize a physical quality of the materials.

Objects are made of one or more materials, such as paper, wood, metal, and wool. But at this age, students do not distinguish between objects and materials.

Get Set for Instruction

Students' experience observing, manipulating, and classifying common objects provides the foundation for much of their later learning. We will be able to help students build concepts related to the properties of objects and materials by providing a variety of experiences:

- observing and describing properties of objects—sizes, shapes, colors, textures, and so on
- comparing objects for their observable similarities and differences
- sorting or grouping objects based on their similarities
- taking common objects apart to examine their components.

Because there are so many objects with interesting properties, we never exhaust the possibilities. Exploring properties helps students build an experiential repertoire and learn the language that goes with it. Such repertoire-building helps novices become proficient.

One key to successful science experiences is to give our students ample opportunities for free exploration. We set out the objects and invite students either to see what they can do with them or to find out how they match. An occasional nudge ("Have you tried using a screen to separate the lima beans from the rice?") may move students into productive interactions that they might otherwise miss.

Assessment

Assessing primary students presents a special challenge. For non-readers or beginning readers, we design simple performance tasks around process skills. We might record students' oral explanations of why things happen. The ability to communicate ideas is more important than the use of specific terms. We should be cautious in assessing a change in the students science vocabularies, stressing how they use a word and place it in context.

Three assessment opportunities follow:

- Have students sort objects into two or more categories. Then set out a new object that does not fit these categories, and observe how students either incorporate it or change their categories.
- Carry a clipboard while observing students during free exploration, and write down snippets of informal conversation relating to student achievement and progress.
- Observe children in their learning centers and note their activities.

━━━ Primary Elementary, Grades K-2 ━━━

Go!
An Example of a Classroom in Action

After her students have engaged in a series of activities involving observing and grouping common objects, Judy Ki sets up several drop boxes in her classroom (a drop box is a box that is open at the top and bottom). She wants her students to spend a few days learning about the sounds associated with various objects. During the activity, the students will drop objects into the box on a table and listen to the sounds as the objects hit the table.

Students work in pairs on opposite sides of the drop box. Each student is given an identical set of objects in a bag: small sponge, lump of clay, clothespin, paper clip, small rubber ball, plastic poker chip, small ball made of aluminum foil, large metal washer, leaf, crumpled piece of paper, penny, and other objects.

A student selects an object from her set and, without letting her partner see it, holds it inside the box, ready to let it drop. She asks her partner, "Ready?" When her partner is ready to listen, he answers, "OK," and she drops the object. Her partner then selects an object from his set and tries to duplicate the sound that he heard.

After several days exploring the sounds that objects make, Ms. Ki asks the pairs of students to group the objects in their sets according to the similar sounds they make. For example, some students put all the objects that make a "thud" together, others put the "bouncing sound" objects together.

Ms. Ki knows that this experience will contribute to the students' listening skills and the development of descriptive vocabulary. Over the next few weeks, she continues to provide new objects and the students bring in objects from home for their drop boxes.

Nature of the Learner

At the middle elementary level, most students are able to organize objects and ideas by single properties and follow examples for recording and organizing data. They begin to interpret data.

Preparing for Science

Materials exist in different states—solid, liquid, and gas. Water and other materials are changed from one form to another by heating or cooling. For example, water (a liquid) becomes ice (a solid) when heat is removed from the liquid. Water becomes vapor (a gas) when heat is added to the water. The state or form of water can be changed by heating or cooling it. The state of other substances can be changed in similar ways.

Nature of Instruction

Many students at this level do not understand that water exists as a gas when it evaporates or reaches the boiling point and vaporizes, but simple investigations with heating and evaporation will help prepare students for understanding later.

Students build concepts related to changes of state through a variety of concrete experiences, such as;
- freezing and melting substances (liquid-solid);

- cooling different liquids and comparing at what temperature they freeze (liquid-solid);
- observing evaporation and condensation (liquid-gas);
- recording how long it takes different liquids to evaporate;
- experimenting to see how different factors affect evaporation; and
- observing sublimation (solid-gas) when a solid goes directly into the gaseous phase.

Assessment

Assessments of student's understanding should keep pace with their progress. Multiple-step tasks replace single-step ones; comparisons and evaluations extend the use of data beyond recording and displaying, and explanations are supported by scientific evidence. For example:
- After the students have had experience with condensation, we might ask them to explain why the bathroom mirror fogs up when someone bathes or takes a shower.
- We challenge students to predict which object will be easiest to change to a liquid—a stick of butter, a wax candle, or a chocolate bar—and to explain why they think so. We may also discuss the materials from which these objects are made.

Middle Elementary, Grades 3-4

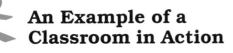

An Example of a Classroom in Action

Sandra Baran shows her students an ice cube and asks them what they think will happen if she places it in a bowl and leaves it there during science class. The students say that the ice cube will melt. Ms. Baran then asks how the ice cube will change when it melts. The students respond that it will become a liquid and will take on the shape of the bowl.

Next, Ms. Baran asks what would cause the ice cube to melt. Some students suggest that the temperature of the room is higher than the temperature at which water freezes. The responses show that the students have an intuitive sense of heat transfer.

Ms. Baran tells the students that they are going to have an ice cube race. She asks what they might do to make the ice melt faster, and lists these suggestions on the board. Then she asks students if an ice cube will melt faster in a plastic cup with water in it (at room temperature) or in a plastic cup with air in it. When she asks where the ice will get heat in order to melt, the students respond, from the air or the water. She encourages the students to make predictions.

Ms. Baran gives each student an ice cube in an empty plastic cup and another one in a plastic cup of water. Then she starts timing the activity.

The students discover that the ice cube in water melts faster. When the students explain their observations, they suggest that the water "heated up" the ice cube more than the air did. Ms. Baran emphasizes the idea that transferring heat energy from the water to the ice cube changed the solid into a liquid.

Some questions Ms. Baran asks are

- where did the ice get the heat needed to melt it?
- which can provide more heat—water or air?

Finally, the class talks about how they could find out if heat travels differently through different substances. Students suggest that they could put ice cubes in different substances such as salt water, sugar water, vinegar, and rubbing alcohol and observe the time it takes for the ice cubes to melt. They decide to try some of these investigations in the future.

Nature of the Learner

Most upper elementary students can follow changes in the sequence of events. They are more skilled at finding information and in recording, synthesizing, and interpreting data. They begin to recognize the relationship between explanation and evidence.

Preparing For Science

A **mixture** is made when two or more substances are combined yet each retains its own properties. Simple mixtures include sand and water, nuts and bolts, coleslaw, and trail mix. Mixtures can be any combination of gases, liquids, and solids.

Sometimes a mixture results in a **solution**. When sugar and water mix, the solid sugar **dissolves** and disappears in the water. Although the solution looks like water, it tastes sweet. Soda water is a solution of carbon dioxide gas in water. Solutions may be **concentrated** or **diluted**, depending upon the amount of the dissolved substance.

Sometimes substances react chemically to form new substances with different properties. In a **chemical reaction**, new materials form, and it may not be possible to retrieve the original materials.

If an Alka-Seltzer tablet is dropped into a glass of water, the tablet fizzes. Fizzing is evidence of change and the formation of a new product.

Mixtures are separated using processes that depend on their different properties. A mixture of Earth materials, such as pebbles, sand, and silt, is separated by sifting the mixture through a series of screens; a mixture of lima beans, peas, and rice is separated by hand. Physical factors used to separate the components of a mixture include gravity, centrifugal force, flotation, filtration, distillation, and magnetic separation. Solutions are also separated by evaporation.

Nature of Instruction

Students build concepts related to mixtures and solutions by

- putting materials together: solids with solids, solids with liquids, liquids with liquids, and so on
- making solutions: solids with liquids (salt or sugar and water)
- chemical reactions: solids with solids and water (calcium chloride and baking soda; baking soda and citric acid in water; calcium chloride and citric acid).

KAREN BUSH HOIBERG

Assessment

Evaluating process skills is accomplished by performing tasks, while open-response questions assess knowledge. We determine overall progress by examining a collection of a student's work. We should always try to provide students with many opportunities to demonstrate their understanding of concepts.

Here are some possibilities:

- Ask students to design a series of tests to determine if the temperature at which water boils changes when various amounts of sugar are added.
- Give students a container filled with a mixture of stones, pebbles, sand, and silt. Ask them to find a way to separate the substances.
- Give students a container of water and dissolved salt. Ask them to remove the salt and determine how much salt was in the water.

SHEILA PELL

An Example of a Classroom in Action

Mary Nelson has planned several days of activities to give her students experience with the concepts of concentration, dilution, and saturation.

First she has her students make a salt and water solution by stirring a teaspoonful (5mL) of table salt (sodium chloride) in a 50 mL glass of water. The students observe and take notes as the salt disappears in the water. They add a second spoonful, then a third, and so on, making the solution more concentrated. At some point, students notice that some of the salt remains at the bottom of the glass and does not dissolve. They speculate about their observation. Ms. Nelson then asks them to pour the solution through filter paper and make additional observa-

tions. On another day, Ms. Nelson repeats the activity with sugar in place of the salt.

Students find there is a point at which solutions cannot dissolve any more of a substance. Ms. Nelson asks the students to compare the concentation of the sugar and salt by discussing the amounts of each that were added.

Later, Ms. Nelson intends to let her students determine what happens when the water is heated before the salt or sugar are added. She asks them to explore ways to remove the salt and sugar from the water by evaporation and to compare the amounts of salt and sugar after evaporation with the amounts used to saturate the glass of water.

Some of the questions Ms. Nelson asks during these activities are
- How can you make a concentrated solution?
- Why is it that the substance dissolved in the solution passes through the filter paper but the undissolved substance does not?
- Why do the substances that go into solution come out of solution?
- Suppose I was mixing orange juice from frozen concentrate and the label on the container said to add four cans of water, but I only added two. How would my orange juice taste? How would it pour? Would the change result in a more concentrated or more dilute drink than the recipe on the can?

Nature of the Learner

Most middle elementary students understand that changing an objects position does not change its size. They continue developing an external reference system and explain changes in position in terms of the interactions that cause them.

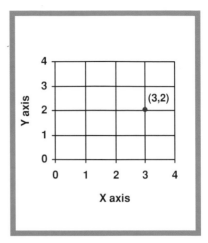

Preparing for Science

A *reference object* is an object that is used to help describe the position of other objects. The *relative position* of an object is its location described relative to a reference object. *Relative motion* is an object's change of position relative to a reference object. We can describe the relative positions of objects through the measurement of direction and distance. These numerical measures are called *coordinates*.

Horizontal and vertical lines form a *rectangular grid* with numbered *rectangular coordinates*, beginning with zero at the lower left corner. It is customary to write the horizontal distance first and the vertical distance second, placing them in parentheses, as in (3,2).

Nature of Instruction

Students are able to build concepts related to position and motion through a variety of experiences such as

- investigating the position and movement of objects
- using reference objects to describe the relative positions of objects
- identifying the relative movement of objects (including classmates) during activities
- examining the changing direction of shadows
- playing games that use rectangular coordinates
- engaging in mapping activities that use rectangular coordinates.

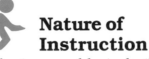

Assessment

As students progress, our assessment of their understanding of science should keep pace. Multiple-step tasks replace single-step ones; comparisons and evaluations extend the use of data beyond recording and displaying, and student explanations can be supported by scientific evidence. Here are some possibilities:

- Have students describe positions of objects relative to a reference object.
- Have students use rectangular coordinates to describe the positions of attractions in an amusement park relative to the entrance.
- Ask students to predict the location of an object on a grid when given its rectangular coordinates.

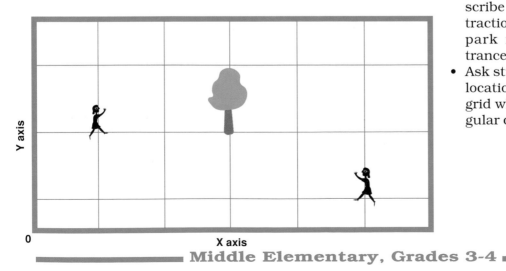

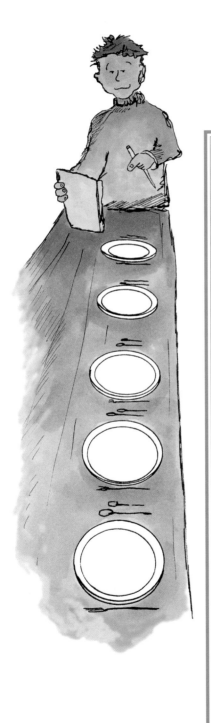

An Example of a Classroom in Action

Marie Gautier has planned a unit on the position and motion of objects. For the first activity, she places two tables—one round and one rectangular—in the center of the classroom. She sets chairs around the tables. At each chair, she puts circles of different colors to represent plates, and representations of a salad fork, a knife, and two spoons.

The students sit in the chairs and look at the utensils across from them and draw what they see. After two minutes, Ms. Gautier asks the students to move to the chair at their right and to draw the same plates and utensils. This continues until all the class has participated in the activity.

In another activity Ms. Gautier's class goes to the playground to observe the relative motion of the Sun by observing and recording shadows of specific objects at different times of the day, and, if possible, at different times of the year.

In a third activity, Ms. Gautier draws a grid on the playground. The students play games on the grid and take part in a playground mapping activity that requires reference to the students' positions on the grid.

After these activities, Ms. Gautier asks her students:
- How would you describe the position of an object (utensils)?
- How did the forks, the knife, and the spoons look as you moved around the table? Why do you think this happened?
- Where was the Sun relative to the object?
- In what direction did the shadow move?
- How will the shadow look in two weeks.
- How would you describe the position of an object on the grid?
- Write directions for locating a specific object on the grid.
- Find as object on the grid using a classmate's directions.

Nature of the Learner

At the upper elementary level, most students observe and describe how substances interact with energy. They are able to follow the transfer of energy from energy source to energy receiver.

Preparing for Science

Energy in the form of light, heat (thermal energy), electricity, and magnetism is intangible, and difficult to define simply and accurately. A simple scientific definition is "Energy is the ability to do work." In other words, you can use energy to bring about certain changes in systems or their surroundings. However, to receive energy, you must have a source, such as wind, the Sun, or fossil fuel.

A charged flashlight dry cell is an **energy source** because chemicals in the dry cell supply energy. The flashlight bulb, which obtains energy from the energy source, is an **energy receiver**.

An **energy chain** is a series of **energy transfers**. For example, when you turn the lights on, electrical energy is transferred to the light bulb's filament, which gives off energy as light and heat to the environment. The energy is provided by a generator, which receives energy from a turbine, which, in turn, has energy transferred to it from very hot, compressed steam. The steam may be produced and heated by coal or oil that burns with oxygen.

Nature of Instruction

Students find the concept of energy use much more concrete and understandable than the scientific definition of energy. They are able to build on earlier experiences with light, heat, and electricity, and develop their understanding of energy through new learning experiences in which they observe, identify, and describe the energy source, energy receiver, and energy transfer. Examples include
- building a flashlight
- adding hot tap water to a glass of cold water and comparing the temperatures just before and just after the hot water was added
- setting up different kinds of electrical circuits (open, closed, in series, in parallel)
- comparing electromagnets that have different numbers of coils of wire wrapped around an iron core.

When students trace energy transfers, they may not recognize subtle changes. However, the study of energy transfer in situations where sources and receivers are easily identified will prepare them for understanding the principle of the conservation of energy.

Assessment

When we assess students, we should focus on tasks that require light, heat, and electrical energy, and identifying an energy source, energy receiver, and energy transfer in each system. Here are some possibilities:
- Give students cardboard "mystery cards" that have hidden wires on the underside connecting various points (use brass brads), and ask students to construct and use a circuit to figure out which points are connected.
- Have students construct and draw a diagram of series and parallel circuits to show the energy source, energy receiver, and energy transfer.
- Have students construct a telegraph that uses electromagnets.

In each case, we might ask students to describe what they did and to explain the results of their actions

NANCY MARRA

An Energy Chain

Coal and oxygen➤flame➤steam➤turbine➤generator➤light bulb➤light and heat

An Example of a Classroom in Action

Pat Jones shows her students two plastic resealable bags—one filled with hot water and the other with cold water. She asks the students to predict what will happen when she pours the hot water into the bag of cold water. The students respond that the hot and cold water will mix. Then Ms. Jones places the two bags so that they are touching each other and asks students to predict the temperature changes in this system in which the hot and cold water interact but do not mix. She asks students to identify the energy source and the energy receiver in this system. The students respond that the hot water is the energy source and the cold water is the energy receiver.

Ms. Jones divides the students into groups of four. She asks each group to measure 80 mL of hot tap water into a 250 mL glass beaker and 80 mL of cold tap water into a 100 mL glass beaker. Each group measures and records the tem-

perature of the cold water and the hot water. Then each group places the 100 mL beaker (cold water) in the 250 mL beaker (hot water). A thermometer remains in both beakers and for 10 minutes, at two-minute intervals, students record the temperature in each beaker.

Ms. Jones asks her students
- How did you make your observations in this investigation?
- How would you describe the energy transfer in this system?
- How would you describe your graph in terms of energy sources and energy receivers during each two-minute interval and during the entire 10 minutes?
- What variables might affect the amount of energy transferred?
- What variables might affect

the rate at which energy is transferred?
- How would each of the following variables affect the outcome of the investigation: The amount of warm and cold water? The starting temperatures? The material and shape of the containers?
- Compare the amount of energy given off by the energy source with the amount of energy taken up by the energy receiver.
- How would the energy transfer and the temperature graph be affected if more hot water than cold water had been used?

PROGRAMS FOR ELEMENTARY SCIENCE

PRIMARY ELEMENTARY - GRADES K-2

Properties of objects and materials

Full Option Science System (FOSS)
Wood, Paper, Fabrics Modules
Three kindergarten-level modules introduce students to the properties of solid objects.

Full Option Science System (FOSS)
Solids and Liquids Modules
Introduces students to the properties of solids and liquids, including aspects affecting changes of state.

Science and Technology for Children (STC)
Solids and Liquids Unit
Students investigate the properties of solids and liquids.

Science for Life and Living (BSCS)
Objects and Properties Unit
Students observe and describe the properties of many objects, then they organize them.

Science Curriculum Improvement Study 3 (SCIS3)
Material Objects Unit
Students study objects, sorting them by their properties.

Position and motion of objects

Full Option Science System (FOSS)
Balance and Motion Module
Introduces primary-level students to the fundamental behavior of objects that balance, spin, or roll.

Insights (EDC)
Balls and Ramps Module
Students explore the properties of balls and some of the factors that affect the way the balls behave.

Science and Technology for Children (STC)
Balancing and Weighing Unit
Students study the relationship between balance and weight. Ways to balance objects are explored.

Science Curriculum Improvement Study 3 (SCIS3)
Interaction and Systems Unit
Students explore the relationship between objects and materials.

Science Curriculum Improvement Study 3 (SCIS3)
Relative Position and Motion Unit
Students explore relative position and motion and graph time/space relationships.

MIDDLE ELEMENTARY - GRADES 3-4

Properties of objects and materials

Full Option Science System (FOSS)
Sound Module
Introduces students to the properties of sounds. Includes the creation of musical instruments.

Full Option Science System (FOSS)
Water Module
Students examine the properties of water. Includes math and graphing techniques.

Great Explorations in Math and Science (GEMS)
Liquid Explorations Unit
Students explore liquids, play a classification game, and observe how substances interact with liquids.

Great Explorations in Math and Science (GEMS)
Involving Dissolving Unit
Students learn about dissolving, evaporation, and crystallization using familiar substances.

Insights (EDC)
Liquids Module
Students explore liquids, compare different liquids, and conduct sinking/floating activities.

Science and Technology for Children (STC)
Sounds Unit
Students investigate sound and how humans use it. Vibrations, pitch, and loudness are studied.

Insights (EDC)
Sound Module
Students study the nature, diversity, and abundance of sounds, and learn about vibrations, pitch, volume, and transmission of sound.

Light, heat, electricity, and magnetism

Full Option Science System (FOSS)
Magnetism/Electricity Module
Introduces magnetism, electricity, and electromagnetism. Includes mathematics and graphing techniques.

Science and Technology for Children (STC)
Electric Circuits Unit
Students explore circuits, construct circuit testers, and investigate conductivity.

PROGRAMS FOR ELEMENTARY SCIENCE

UPPER ELEMENTARY - GRADES 5-6

Properties and changes of properties in motion

Full Option Science System (FOSS)
Mixtures/Solutions Module
Introduces students to mixtures, solutions, and simple chemical changes.

Great Explorations in Math and Science (GEMS)
Chemical Reactions Unit
Students mix chemicals that bubble, change color, get hot, and produce gas, heat, and an odor. They experiment to determine the origin of heat in a chemical reaction.

Science and Technology for Children (STC)
Chemical Tests Unit
Students study the physical properties of white powders, including their solubility and crystallization.

Motion and forces

Full Option Science System (FOSS)
Levers and Pulleys Module
Introduces students to motion and force using leaves and pulleys. Uses mathematics and graphs.

Transfer of energy

Full Option Science System (FOSS)
Solar Energy Module
Students study heat, its effect upon different surfaces, how it can be measured, and efficient solar homes.

Great Explorations in Math and Science (GEMS)
Hot Water & Warm Homes from Sunlight Unit
Students build solar houses and hot waterheaters and experiment with heat produced by sunlight.

Science Curriculum Improvement Study 3 (SCIS3)
Energy Sources Unit
Students explore sources of energy. They study potential energy and kinetic energy.

See appendix D for addresses

OTHER TOPICS COVERED BY STANDARD B

Light, heat, electricity, and magnetism for levels K-4 and *Motions and forces* for levels 5-8 have not been illustrated. The following resources contain information and activities that cover these topics.

Topic: describing matter
Go to: http://www.scilinks.org/
Code: PAE02

Topic: forces and motion
Go to: http://www.scilinks.org/
Code: PAE03

Topic: energy
Go to: http://www.scilinks.org/
Code: PAE04

Anthony, Joan L. (1994, February). Race Car Rally. *Science & Children, 31* (5), 26-29.

Baird, Hugh. (1994, November/December). Keying out Banana Splits. *Science Scope, 18* (3), 12-16.

Barry, Dana Malloy. (1990, September). Fat Burgers. *Science Scope, 14* (1), 34-36.

Beichner, Robert J. (1990, May). Paper Cup Magnetism. *Science Scope, 13,* (8), 18-19.

Chaille, Christine, and Britain, Lory. (1991). *The Young Child as Scientist: A Constructivist Approach to Early Childhood Science Education.* New York: Harper Collins.

Conrad, III, William H. (1992, November/December). Create a Polarized Light Show. *Science and Children, 30* (3), 24-26.

Dana, Thomas M., and Perkins, Rhonda, and Ledford, Kelly, and St. Pierre, Melissa. (1993, April). Fun-filled Physics. *Science and Children, 30* (7), 28-31.

Domel, Rue. (1993, October). You Can Teach About Acid Rain. *Science and Children, 31 (2),* 25-28.

Fowler, Marilyn. (1992, October). Slime Factory. *Science Scope, 16* (2), 20-22.

Fowler, Marilyn. (1990, September). Glurch Meets Oobleck. *Science Scope, 14* (1), 21-23.

Hajda, Joey, and Hajda, Lisa B. (1994, November/December). Sparking Interest in Electricity. *Science Scope, 18* (3), 36-39.

Hartman, Dean. (1992, September). Electric Mystery Boxes. *Science Scope, 16* (7), 26-28.

Janulaw, Al. (1993, November/December). The Magnetic Pendulum. *Science Scope, 17* (3), 50-52.

Jones, Richard. (1995, October). How Big, How Tall? The Scaling Principle Answers. *Science Scope, 19* (2), 22-26.

Moore, Virginia S., and Kaszas, William J. (1995, February). All Aboard! For a Lesson on Magnetic Levitated Trains. *Science and Children, 32* (5), 15-18, 47.

Papacosta, Pan. (1991, May). Electromagnet Dragnet. *Science Scope, 14* (8), 18-21.

Park, John C. (1992, April). Copter Gun Explorations. *Science Scope, 15* (7), 24-26.

Scarnati, James T. (1993, March). Tracks Revisited. *Science and Children, 30* (6), 23-25.

Scheckel, Larry. (1993, November/December). How to Make Density Float. *Science and Children. 31* (3), 30-33.

Spurlin, Quincy. (1995, January). Put Science in a Bag. *Science and Children, 32* (4), 19-22.

Stiles, John R. (1992, November/December). Mealworms: A Year-Round Science Project. *Science Scope, 16* (3), 36-39.

Stone, Marla. (1991, January). The Unseen Bottom. *Science Scope, 14* (4), 32-35.

Sumrall, William J., and Criglow, Judy. (1995, March). The "Scoop" on Science Data. *Science and Children, 32* (6), 36-39, 44.

Truho, Gail. (1993, September). Testing Gum, Two, Three .... *Science and Children, 31* (1), 19-21.

Wallace, John, and Warner, Janise. (1996, February). Words, Words, Words. *Science and Children, 33* (5), 17-19.

Wilson, Roger B. (1993, May). Flinking: Neither Floating Nor Sinking. *Science Scope, 16* (8), 20-21.

The full text to most of these resources is available on NSTA's supplementary *Resources for the Road CD-ROM.*

LIFE SCIENCE

INTRODUCTION

All living things move, seek nourishment, breathe, and reproduce, and they accomplish these activities in a wide variety of ways. A plant's movement, for example, is different from an animal's; an elephant's movement is different from a monkey's. Each type of organism has structures that enable it to function in unique and specific ways to obtain food, reproduce, and survive.

Children's natural interest in their surroundings is often expressed as a fascination with living things. From sow bugs and ants to puppies and kittens to trees and plants, living things have an inherent attraction that continues throughout students' elementary school years.

Because elementary school children are good observers, grades K-6 are a good time for them to use their powers of observation to discover similarities and differences in the characteristics and behavior of living organisms. It is a time for us to encourage students to look closely, watch carefully over a period time, and think about how organisms are alike and different.

For example, students see how an animal moves, understand how the construction of its body enables this movement, and decide what is distinctive about the way it moves.

The Life Science Standard for grades K-4 focuses on three aspects of living organisms: their characteristics, their life cycles, and their environments. The Standard for grades 5-8 includes some beginning explorations into the broader ideas of populations and ecosystems.

Research suggests that students in grades K-6 gradually develop an understanding of the interactions between organisms and between these organisms and their environment. Thus, the content ideas presented in this section follow a progressive sequence in which more advanced ideas (such as recognizing patterns of interaction in ecosystems) builds on a foundation of prior ideas about individual organisms. Throughout the elementary grades, giving students direct experience with living organisms is desirable in school, at home, and in other settings. It is important that, throughout the elementary grades, students be allowed to have direct experience with living organisms at school, at home, and in other settings.

CONTENT STANDARD C

C | K-4
*As a result of activities in grades K-4, all students should develop understanding of
- **The characteristics of organisms**
- **Life cycles of organisms**
- Organisms and environments

5-8

As a result of their activities in grades 5-8, all students should develop understanding of
- Structure and function in living systems
- Reproduction and heredity
- Regulation and behavior
- **Populations and ecosystems**
- Diversity and adaptations of organisms

* Bolded statements are discussed in the text

Nature of the Learner

Primary level students are highly egocentric, but they are beginning to work in partnership with other students. They recognize the needs of other people and of animals and plants.

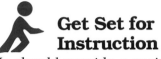

Get Ready for Science

Individual plants and animals live where they have adapted to local conditions. Senses help living organisms detect conditions in the external environment. This information influences their behavior. For example, a lion uses external clues to help him hunt. Behavior is also influenced by internal clues. When we are hungry, we seek food. When we are cold, we try to warm ourselves.

The place that provides the optimum space, food, water, oxygen, and other substances as well as suitable temperature and light is the organisms *habitat.* The frog, for example, needs a wet, or at least a damp, habitat. Its range of tolerance for water availability is narrow which limits its choice of locale. A frog's skin dries out easily, as does the jelly-like cover of frog eggs. The gill-breathing tadpoles cannot survive more than a few minutes without water.

Get Set for Instruction

We should provide a variety of experiences to maximize students' natural curiosity and interest in living organisms. Observations can take place in the classroom and in the field and include:

- Exploring a variety of plants and animals; students should also take on tasks associated with the care, feeding, and maintenance of living organisms.
- Assembling a collection of structures associated with living organisms such as bones, shells, leaves, nests, and cones. The objects can later be sorted.
- Identifying and comparing the various environments in which animals and plants are found naturally.
- Creating murals or constructing models of animals and plants in their environments.
- Discussing the needs of living organisms, then identifying characteristics that help them meet their needs—What needs do all organisms share? Which needs are more specific? Do plants and animals need the same conditions?
- Making masks to be used in role-playing the behavior of animals.

Assessment

The lack of sophistication and reading skills of our primary elementary students present challenges in designing assessments. Here are some possibilities:

- Have students create a mural or diorama depicting one or more environments. Students' illustration of living organisms within the mural reflects their understanding of the organism/environment relationship. Students should identify specific characteristics of these organisms.
- Present a variety of living organisms (or pictures of them) from familiar environments to the class, and have students sort them according to the environments in which they occur naturally.
- Observe students during free exploration. Their interest, motivation, and sophistication in exploring can be used to gauge their understanding and the quality of their thinking.
- Encourage role-playing activities. Using appropriate masks and props, students can illustrate their understanding of the behavior and lifestyle of a variety of living organisms.

━━━━━ **Primary Elementary, Grades K-2** ━━━━━

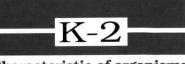

Go! An Example of a Classroom in Action

Harry Kelly's class has been studying various animals that live around the school grounds. Today, Mr. Kelly has brought a small mammal, a hamster, into the classroom. He guides the students on how to care for the hamster, helping them set up an appropriate cage, keep it clean, teaching them how to feed the hamster a proper diet.

As the students care for the hamster, Mr. Kelly guides them by taking notes on its characteristics and behavior. Each day, students discuss what the animal does and how it accomplishes what it needs to do.

After the instruction on the care and housing of a small mammal, Mr. Kelly introduces other animals into the classroom. Soon, there are containers of grasshoppers, caterpillars, earthworms, and so forth.

The children learn about the different environments needed for each animal and what kind of care, including food, is required. They observe how each animal behaves, what, when, and how it eats and when it sleeps. They keep journals in which they draw pictures of the animals engaged in several activities.

It is not long before the children have discovered a good deal about the diversity of living organisms as well as the similarities in animals needs (such as sleep and food). They have also learned some important concepts about the care and keeping of animals for the purpose of study.

Nature of the Learner

Most middle elementary students are able to compare objects by their multiple characteristics and organize objects and ideas into broad concepts, first on the basis of single properties, later by multiple properties (one at a time).

Preparing for Science

Biodiversity is the word used to describe the variety of life on Earth. A fundamental understanding of this concept can be gained by identifying similarities and differences between species in a habitat as well as between the great diversity of habitats around the world. Students gain understanding by recognizing the different characteristics of species that exist today and those that lived in the past; recognizing that each species lives in a specific and fairly uniform environment; learn-

ing about the way biological evolution and adaptation account for diversity; and identifying examples where the extinction of a species occurs because of environmental change and nonadaptive behaviors.

Nature of Instruction

Our students begin to learn about biodiversity through a variety of instructional experiences that focus on the similarities and differences between organisms. Some possible experiences are:

- Using a variety of pictures of animals, students discuss their similarities and differences.
- Depending on local resources, students visit a variety of ecosystems such as ponds, grassy areas, wetlands, coral reefs, deserts, and so on to identify different species. We talk with students about the interac-

tion and dependence of the species in an environment. We integrate this exploration with powerful ideas in social studies. For example, because human culture is closely linked to the idea of biodiversity, cultures are, in part, shaped by the environment.

Valuable learning happens when students make sense of their own experiences and develop new understanding. We need to plan activities that enable students to answer their own questions about the characteristics of organisms in an environment and give them ample opportunity to exchange ideas with one another.

Teaching a complex idea, such as biodiversity, takes considerable time. If students are forced to move ahead too fast they will resort to memorizing information and forcing it into their current ideas, rather than changing and adjusting their current ideas to embrace the new concept.

Assessment

Ask students to express their understanding of biodiversity:

- Observe students recording information and listen to their discussions as they look at diversity in a specific environment. Note what they find to be important observations, what questions they raise, and

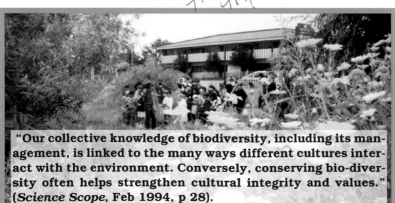

"Our collective knowledge of biodiversity, including its management, is linked to the many ways different cultures interact with the environment. Conversely, conserving bio-diversity often helps strengthen cultural integrity and values." (*Science Scope*, Feb 1994, p 28).

how they them.

- Have students debate the reasons why certain species are extinct. Assess the quality of their arguments—their evidence and how they have organized evidence to make a logical case for their point of view. Note especially whether their evidence is supported by observations of the characteristics of the organisms.

- Use anecdotal records and students' journals to assess what each student has accomplished.

ALITA D. FREY

An Example of a Classroom in Action

Our teaching strategies may be different, but we need to include the following:

- A framework for developing student understanding.
- An effort to create a community of learners.
- An attempt to guide and facilitate learning by supporting inquiry.
- A challenge to students to take responsibility for their own learning and to work collaboratively.
- An environment of equity.
- A teacher model of inquiry, curiosity, openness to new ideas, and skepticism.
- The flexibility to change plans based on ongoing assessment of learning.

- A feeling of physical, mental, and emotional safety in the learning environment.
- Time for students to reflect.

All these strategies are embedded in the following scenario that describes students in a classroom exploring the characteristics of organisms.

Barbara Laub's class has been working outside the classroom in groups, each group using string to cordon off a square foot of the environment they are studying. Each square foot is studied as a microhabitat. Each will differ depending on what is available: a local field, a pond, or a well-traveled pathway.

Students discuss what they see and hear, and they record their observations in words and pictures that describe the characteristics and quantities of animal and plant life.

When they return to the classroom, members of each group talk about the data they gathered. They put it in a format that can be shared visually and orally. Visual representations are hung on the wall, and all students go on a "wisdom walk" looking for similarities, patterns, and differences between organisms studied in the microhabitats. Ms. Laub asks the students what influenced either the abundance of different organisms or the lack of biodiversity. She challenges them to give evidence supporting their ideas.

Nature of the Learner

Middle elementary students organize objects and ideas into broad concepts, first on the basis of single properties, later on the basis of multiple properties (one at a time). They record data and keep simple journals.

Preparing for Science

The *life cycle* is an important principle in biology. It represents the stages an organism passes through from its own birth to the birth of the next generation.

All organisms living on Earth, from the simplest to the most complex, grow and change from birth until they are adults and are ready to reproduce. Organisms are capable of transforming raw materials from the environment (food, water, minerals) into more or less identical copies of themselves. All living organisms have life cycles, but details differ for different organisms.

Nature of Instruction

We can help students learn to understand this principle through a variety of experiences, such as

- planting seeds; growing the seedlings to maturity;

JANEY YENOR

watching the plants flower; watching the flowers become pollinated and change to pods (fruits) filled with seeds like those originally planted; and then seeing the "new" seeds begin the cycle again
- watching an animal give birth, seeing the young grow to adulthood, and watching some of those adults give birth to a new set of young

Assessment

To assess students' understanding of the life cycle, we might try activities like the following:

- Ask students to draw a sequence of stages that shows an example of a complete cycle. They may start anywhere within the cycle (for example, with the adult organism rather than the organism at birth). We might begin by asking students whether any starting place would be appropriate (and why or why not). Their responses will reveal how well they understand the idea that a cycle begins again when the process is transferred to another organism.
- Ask students to sequence sets of cards that depict the stages in the life cycle of three different organisms and to talk about the similarities and differences in the sequences.

Middle Elementary, Grades 3-4

An Example of a Classroom in Action

In Alice Borden's class, the children have been growing FAST plants for several days. They have been measuring the height of the plants, writing descriptions of how the plants change each day, and drawing in their journals. While the plants grow, the students have been reading relevant books from the library.

In several more days, the students will harvest the seeds from the adult plants. They will observe and study them, then plant them to start another life cycle.

As the children carry out their study, Mrs. Borden moves from group to group, posing questions and assessing the children's understanding of what they see. She adjusts the instruction as a result of her assessment of their responses.

NOTE: FAST plants are available from Carolina Biological Supply Co., 2700 York Road, Burlington, NC 27215 (Telephone 919-584-0381).

Some of the questions Mrs. Borden asks on different days are:
- What is the best way to keep a record of the changes we observe from day to day?
- How can we take our records and organize the information to explain to someone else what we have learned?
- Describe the life cycle of a plant we studied.
- Make a drawing of the plant.
- How is our knowing about the life cycles of plants important to us?

Nature of the Learner

Most upper elementary students are able to recognize the life cycles of organisms. They begin to identify populations and ecosystems, recognize diversity, and use the understanding of ecological concepts they have developed in everyday experiences.

Preparing for Science

A **population** consists of all the individuals of a species inhabiting a given area. An **ecosystem** comprises all the populations living together in an area and the vegetative and physical matter with which they interact.

Populations of organisms can be categorized according to the function they serve in an ecosystem. For example, plants are **producers** because they make their own food. Animals are **consumers** because they eat plants and other animals. Organisms that break down dead plants and animals are called **decomposers**.

A deeper understanding of the concepts requires some understanding of the energy flow between members of a **community** (interacting populations in a common location) and of factors that affect the balance of an ecosystem. **Food webs** express the relationships between producers, consumers, and decomposers in an ecosystem.

Nature of Instruction

Students learn about populations and ecosystems through a variety of instructional experiences. Plan field trips to different environments such as local streams, ponds, rivers, wildlife areas, or your school grounds, so that students can investigate the populations and ecosystems found there. Have students discuss what they see or keep journals of their observations. Ask them to look at small areas within each environment and map what they observe.

Students can note the kinds of animal and plant life and their location, the sources of water and energy, and interactions between organisms.

Assessment

To determine whether students understand the idea of an ecosystem, its components, and the factors that affect it, we might do the following:

- Using live creatures, have students replicate an environment that will sustain life within the classroom setting.
- Have students draw and talk about the physical factors of a particular ecosystem.
- Ask students to draw or make a model of a food web.
- Have a panel of students discuss or debate issues related to factors that limit or encourage the growth of populations. One possibility would be a discussion of a rain forest and its stakeholders.
- Have students keep written journals or create original field guides. Be sure they know before they start that you will use their work to assess their learning.

> **SAFETY NOTE:**
> **Be sure to check the rules of the site BEFORE the class takes the trip or hike.**

An Example of a Classroom in Action

After discussing naturally occurring changes that the students observed in their community, Sam Kim's sixth-grade decided to set up an experiment in their school yard that would demonstrate an ecosystem. The class marked off four equal grassy rectangles, 1 m by 1.5 m, two under a large oak tree and two in the corner of the school yard in full sunlight. The space between each pair of rectangles measured 1 m. Each member of the class recorded a description of each rectangle which included color, the amount of grass, number and type of insects, and air and ground temperatures in the Sun and in the shade.

Every third day, for three weeks, the students watered two of the rectangles using 3.5 L of water for each rectangle. Each time they watered, they recorded their observations.

After the three-week period, students were able to observe changes in both plants and animals. They also compared the watered areas with those not watered and the rectangles in the shade with the rectangles in full sunlight.

The students discussed the following questions:

- What happened to the ecosystem when water was added?
- How were the areas affected that were not watered?
- How were the areas affected by the Sun?
- What can we tell about the environmental changes?
- How did these changes affect the populations existing in this system?
- What methods of adaptation did we see?
- How can we apply what we have learned about this ecosystem to the ones we see around us every day?

After time for discussion and reflection, the students work independently, in pairs, to illustrate what they have learned. They know they are expected to present their ideas to the rest of the class. They explore possible formats for their presentations. Some prepare written reports; others make a cartoon strip of their observations. One group tries a video presentation. Mr. Kim will use the presentations to assess the quality of his students' understanding.

PROGRAMS FOR ELEMENTARY SCIENCE

PRIMARY ELEMENTARY - GRADES K-2

The characteristics of organisms

Full Option Science System (FOSS)
Trees Module
Students explore the characteristics of a tree during the school year.

Full Option Science System (FOSS)
Animals 2 by 2 Module
Kindergarten students study the observable characteristics of animals.

Science and Technology for Children (STC)
Organisms Unit
Students maintain freshwater and woodland habitats to study the diversity of living organisms.

Life cycles of organisms

Full Option Science System (FOSS)
Insects Module
Students study the structures and behavior of selected insects and their life cycles.

Full Option Science System (FOSS)
New Plants Module
Students study responses to environmental conditions of the selected plants, diversity, and life cycles.

Life Lab
Explorations Unit
Students explore water, soil, plants, and animals as they develop a garden.

Life Lab
Diversity and Cycles Unit
Students investigate the characteristics, growth, and cycles of plants, animals, and Earth materials.

Life Lab
Changes Unit
Students study the water cycle, air, and food chains.

Science and Technology for Children (STC)
Life Cycle of Butterflies Unit
Introduces students to the life cycle of the painted lady butterfly.

Science Curriculum Improvement Study 3 (SCIS3)
Life Cycles Unit
Students explore the life cycles of various plant and animal organisms.

MIDDLE ELEMENTARY - GRADES 3-4

Organisms and environments

Full Option Science System (FOSS)
Structures of Life Module
Introduces students to a selected number of plants and crayfish to study their responses to environmental changes.

Science and Technology for Children (STC)
Animal Studies Unit
Students learn about animals' needs and adaptations by investigating frogs, crabs, and snails.

The characteristics of organisms

Full Option Science System (FOSS)
Human Body Module
Students study their bone and muscular structures and how the two function to create movement.

Life Lab
Structure-Function Unit
Students use their gardens to study the structures of plants and animals in a habitat.

Life Lab
Connections Unit
Students study interactions in and around their gardens: food webs, nutrient conservation, and ecosystems.

Life cycle of organisms

Science and Technology for Children (STC)
Plant Growth and Development Unit
Students grow plants to learn about life cycles and the interdependence of living organisms.

UPPER ELEMENTARY - GRADES 5-6

Populations and ecosystems

Full Option Science System (FOSS)
Environments Module
Introduces students to environmental factors that affect living organisms. Includes exploring levels of tolerance.

Life Lab
Change Over Time Unit
Using a garden, students investigate adaptation, changes in season, energy, soil, weather, and climate.

Science and Technology for Children (STC)
Ecosystems Unit
Students study the interdependence of living and nonliving elements in their environment and maintain a terrarium and an aquarium.

Science and Technology for Children (STC)
Experiments with Plants Unit
Students test variables that affect the life, health, and reproduction of plants.

Science for Life and Living (BSCS)
Ecosystems and Resources Unit
Students make decisions about how to manage ecosystems for the benefit of plants and animals.

Science Curriculum Improvement Study 3 (SCIS3)
Ecosystems Unit
Students study the factors that make up an ecosystem.

Science Curriculum Improvement Study 3 (SCIS3)
Populations Unit
Students study the interrelationships of organisms and populations.

Structure and function of organisms

Full Option Science System (FOSS)
Structures of Life Module
Introduces students to a number of plants and crayfish to study their structures and how these enable them to survive.

Regulation and behavior

Great Explorations in Math and Science (GEMS)
Earthworms Unit
Students record pulse rates of earthworms to discover their response to different temperatures. Results are graphed.

See Appendix D for addresses

LIFE SCIENCE

OTHER TOPICS COVERED BY STANDARD C

Organisms and the environment for levels K-4, and *Structure and function in living organisms, Reproduction and heredity, Regulation and behavior,* and *Diversity and adaptations of organisms* for levels 5-8 have not been illustrated. The following resources contain information and activities that cover these topics.

SCI/LINKS
THE WORLD'S A CLICK AWAY

Topic: characteristics of living things
Go to: http://www.scilinks.org/
Code: PAE05

Topic: growth and development
Go to: http://www.scilinks.org/
Code: PAE06

Topic: populations, communities, and ecosystems
Go to: http://www.scilinks.org/
Code: PAE07

Topic: genetics
Go to: http://www.scilinks.org/
Code: PAE08

RESOURCES FOR THE ROAD

Bollwinkel, Carl W. (1990, November/December). Keeping Pace with Snails. *Science Scope.* 14 (3), 30-32.

Goh, Ngoh-Khang; Wan, Yoke-Kum; Chia, Lian-Sai. (1993, September). Simply Photosynthesis. *Science and Children.* 31 (1), 32-34.

Grambo, Gregory. (1995, May). Raising Butterflies in Your Classroom. *Science Scope.* 18 (8), 16-18.

Ma, Peggy R. (1993, October). On Golden Pond. *Science Scope.* 17 (2), 10-13.

Moody, Dwight. (1993, May). Take Flight with Dragons and Damsels. *Science and Children.* 30 (8), 12-15.

Olien, Rebecca. (1993, September). Worm Your Way to Science. *Science and Children.* 31 (1), 25-27.

Shimabukuro, Mary A., and Fearing, Vickie. (1993, May). How Does Your Garlic Grow? *Science and Children.* 30 (8), 8-11.

The full text to most of these resources is available on NSTA's supplementary *Resources for the Road CD-ROM.*

From earliest times, humans have looked at the Earth and sky with wonder, trying to find explanations for what they saw. Today, we have learned more about our solar system from our own experiences, and from the great wealth of information available to us. Together, these two ways of learning help us to understand the world around us.

We know that young children are naturally curious about their world and the living organisms within it. Non living materials like rocks, rivers, stars, and snow also offer opportunities for observation by which students develop an early understanding of Earth and the solar system.

In grades K-4, student learning about Earth and sky occurs primarily by making observations as they explore, collect, describe, and record information. Students investigate the properties of water, rocks, minerals, and soil. We guide them in observing natural changes of all kinds, including cyclical changes, such as the movement of the Sun and moon, and variable changes, like the weather.

The Earth and Space Science Standard for levels 5-8 focuses on the structure of the Earth system, Earth's history, and Earth in the solar system. Students' increased experience and sophistication allow us to introduce the concept of systems, including Earth's four major interacting systems: the geosphere, hydrosphere, atmosphere, and biosphere. The students work with models to explain Earth and solar system phenomena, such as the rock cycle and the water cycle.

Students investigate the interactions between Earth materials to learn about weathering, erosion, deposition and the landforms that result from such processes. A number of the concepts in this Standard, such as the explanations of moving lithospheric plates and cloud formation, are intended for grades 7 and 8.

CONTENT STANDARD D

D

K-4
* As a result of their activities in grades K-4, all students should develop an understanding of
- **Properties of earth materials**
- **Objects in the sky**
- Changes in earth and sky

5-8
As a result of their activities in grades 5-8, all students should develop an understanding of
- **Structure of the earth system**
- Earth's history
- Earth in the solar system

* Bolded statements are discussed in the text

Reprinted with persmission from the *National Science Education Standards*. ©1996 National Academy of Sciences. Courtesy of the National Academy Press, Washington, D.C.

Nature of the Learner

Most students at this level are able to communicate their observations and comparisons to others. They make simple comparisons between objects. With guidance, they will be able to group and order objects on the basis of a single characteristic.

Get Ready for Science

Earth materials are rocks, soils, fossil fuels, water, and the gases in Earth's atmosphere. Earth's surface also includes living organisms, but they are not considered Earth materials.

The various Earth materials have properties that make them useful to us in different ways. Soils vary, but

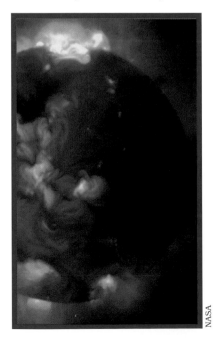

are usually able to support plants. Earth materials are used for building, as sources of fuel, and for growing plants.

Get Set for Instruction

We need to give our students a variety of concrete experiences that enable them to learn about the properties of Earth materials through observation. Here are some examples:

- When students observe and describe the properties of rocks, they will begin to see that some are made up of a single substance, but most are made up of several substances (minerals).
- By collecting rocks and observing vegetation, they will become aware that soil varies in color, texture, and fertility from place to place.
- By visiting an appropriate outdoor study site on a regular basis, students will

come to understand that Earth's surface is constantly changing.
- Show students areas where erosion is occurring.

Assessment

Activities such as grouping and sequentially ordering Earth materials give us opportunities to assess students' skills and understanding of concepts. For example:

- Ask students to group a variety of rocks according to one of their properties, such as color, pattern (plain or striated), buoyancy, or layering.
- Challenge students to find out which type of soil, clay, sand, or humus,
  a) allows the most water to pass through it
  b) filters water most effectively
  c) is best for growing bean plants
  d) crumbles most easily when dry.

Primary Elementary, Grades K-2

Go!
An Example of a Classroom in Action

In Jim Murphy's class, students have been studying the physical properties of Earth materials. Over the past few weeks, they have used hand lenses to gain a close-up view of small rocks, soils, and grains of sand collected from a local beach. Students discussed the similarities and differences between these materials. Their observations sparked various questions. Mr. Murphy asks:

- How do particles of sand and dirt differ from each other?
- Which particles would make the dirt better for growing plants?
- Can dirt turn into rocks? Can rocks turn into dirt?
- Are all grains of sand the same size?

Mr. Murphy selects one of the questions and has his students discuss how a scientist might approach finding the answer.

Mr. Murphy selects a question about the size of the grains of sand because this inquiry can be completed within a reasonable time-frame and requires the use of scientific tools (sieves). He also likes the fact that his students can make use of the sand samples they had collected during the warmer months.

He demonstrates the use of a set of sieves and allows the students to examine them. Then he asks them to think of questions that might be answered by using the sieves. He accepts all reasonable suggestions, such as:

- Are dirt particles bigger than sand particles?
- Do different beaches have sand of different sizes?

He then supplies student groups with sets of sieves and challenges them to sort the grains of sand. He offers sand from two different sources. As the students will discover, one sample is mostly coarse grained; the other, mostly fine grained.

When the students have completed their inquiry, Mr. Murphy asks the groups to share their findings. He challenges them to think of different ways to describe their results. One group displays its data as a pictograph. Another group uses a bar graph. A third presents its findings in cartoon frames.

Mr. Murphy encourages the students to venture beyond concrete observations and draw inferences from their observations.

He asks his students to think of additional questions that would form the basis for particle sorting, such as:

- Are some particles magnetic?
- Do any particles float?
- Will some particles react with vinegar?

Experiences like this one, driven by students' questions, have proved a powerful tool for meeting the goals that Mr. Murphy had set at the beginning of the year.

Nature of the Learner

Most middle elementary students are able to make and record sequential observations and identify simple patterns. With guidance from their teacher, they are able to observe cyclic changes (such as the seasons and the phases of the Moon).

Preparing for Science

Objects in the sky show patterns of movement. The Sun appears to move across the sky in the same way every day, but its path changes slowly over the seasons. The Moon moves across the sky much in the way the Sun does, but its shape seems to change from day to day in a cycle that lasts about a month.

Weather is also a sky phenomenon, varying from day to day and changing over the seasons. Weather can be described quantitatively through temperature, wind direction and speed, and amount of precipitation. An analysis of various measurements, together with careful observations of patterns, makes weather predictions possible

Nature of Instruction

By observing the day and night sky on a regular basis at dif-ferent times, students will learn to identify cyclic change and to look for patterns. Involve students in some of the following activities:

- Each evening, students draw the Moon's shape on a calendar, note when it is visible (day/night), and keep a log of the Moon's color for a period of time. Seeing both the Sun and the Moon in the sky on the same day helps to dispel any notion that one substitutes for the other.

- Students will discover patterns of weather changes during the year by keeping a journal in which they draw daily weather pictures or by creating simple charts and graphs from the data they collect.

Assessment

When assessing what students know about objects in the sky, we stress the skills students have acquired in observing and describing, and how well they base their ex-

NASA

planations on their observations.

- Arranging out-of-sequence images puts to good use the middle elementary students' abilities to place objects in logical order. These images may include the phases of the Moon, satellite images of terrestrial weather patterns and seasonal changes, and changes in living organisms.

- Students keep a log that reflects some sequential observations. This includes observations of the phases of the Moon, temperature changes, wind direction, amount of precipitation, and other planetary events. If students track the data for an extended period, the log may be useful to them in uncovering patterns and cycles based on observations.

- Students use weather data to make their own weather predictions. With temperature, humidity, sky cover, and wind direction, they will be able to make tentative forecasts.

- Students interpret information from the weather page in *USA TODAY*.

Middle Elementary, Grades 3-4

An Example of a Classroom in Action

Shaun Brown finds that lessons are most successful when she encourages her students to construct knowledge for themselves. Today, her class is learning about the phases of the Moon and attempting to develop explanations for them.

The students have been observing the Moon each night for the past two months and drawing pictures of what they have seen. Ms. Brown holds up some of the pictures of the different phases of the Moon.

Ms. Brown then distributes calendar pages and has the students place their pictures on the calendar.

The students continue to gather Moon data for another month, adding their own observations to the calendar pages. When they have collected several months' worth of data, Ms. Brown challenges them with the following questions:

- Does the full Moon appear on the same date each month? Is there a pattern?
- How many days are there between each half Moon and the next half Moon? Between each first-quarter Moon and the next first-quarter Moon?
- Can you uncover a pattern in the appearance of the half Moon or first-quarter Moon? Is it different from a full-Moon pattern?

Nature of the Learner

Most upper elementary students understand Earth's shape and its position in the solar system. They continue to improve at sequencing events. They begin to understand dynamic processes and the interaction of several components.

Preparing for Science

Earth is made up of several layers, each with its own composition and properties. The **lithosphere** includes the **crust** and part of the **upper mantle** and is broken into large sections known as **plates.** These float on the molten rock of the upper mantle which pushes and pulls the plates, causing them to collide, producing earthquakes, volcanoes and mountains. The next deepest layer is the **lower mantle** which surrounds Earth's **core.**

Surface features are worn down by **weathering.** Soil, sand, and small rocks, created by weathering are transported by wind and water. This is called **erosion.** Weathered and eroded rocks produce sediments that are gradually buried, compacted, and subjected to great pressure and heat. Over long periods of time these changed sediments form new rock which may be raised back to the surface and eroded again. This process is called the **rock cycle.**

Another cycle of change is known as the **water cycle**. Surface water evaporates as water vapor. When this invisible vapor cools, it condenses as liquid water. Clouds are composed of water that has condensed on very small particles of dust. When enough water condenses, the droplets fall to Earth as precipitation.

Water flows both above and below ground, and as it moves, it seeps into the soil and dissolves and transports substances. The water collects as groundwater that discharges into bodies of water like streams, rivers, and lakes. Eventually, the water runs into oceans and some of it evaporates, leaving behind the materials that had been dissolved in, it such as salt.

Weather and climate are strongly affected by water. On Earth's surface, the ability of water to hold large amounts of heat moderates temperatures. In the atmosphere, the upper surfaces of clouds reflect sunlight back into space, while the lower surfaces reflect back to Earth the heat that has radiated up from Earth's surface.

Earth's atmosphere is a mixture of different gases, including nitrogen, oxygen, carbon dioxide, and water vapor. The atmosphere has changed over Earth's history, largely because of the actions of living organisms.

Nature of Instruction

Most Earth-shaping events occur on such a large scale and in such inaccessible places that it is rarely possible for our students to experience them directly. Generally we use models—small, simplified representations of the large-scale objects and events—to help students understand the larger processes.

Assessment

Student understanding is measured by traditional and alternate assessment techniques, such as:

- Providing construction materials and asking the students to make models representing the structural aspects of Earth's systems. Include cross-sections of Earth, scale models of land forms, and maps of plate boundaries.
- Giving the students descriptions and photographs of land forms and asking them to describe the geologic processes responsible for forming these features.
- Asking students to make a chart illustrating the rock cycle, attaching samples of appropriate rocks.
- Having students construct a model of the water cycle that shows evaporation and condensation. Students should identify and describe each process.

Upper Elementary, Grades 5-6

An Example of a Classroom in Action

Maria Cantata's class is working with small models, similar to stream tables, to learn about how some landforms are created.

Because her students are not yet familiar with stream tables, Ms. Cantata first introduces some procedures for preparing and using small models. The students learn that they must have a container for collecting runoff water and newspapers for absorbing spillage. Ms. Cantata tells students to think about how to prepare the Earth materials, position the water source, and so on.

As a preliminary activity, the students work, in groups, running water for a specified length of time through sand, soil, and gravel and observing the results. Ms. Cantata asks the students to discuss and compare their results, using graphs and drawings.

Next, Ms. Cantata involves students in an open-ended investigation in which they generate questions and formulate hypotheses. She provides the materials that students will need to generate evidence that may or may not support their ideas.

The students' questions suggest various inquiry possibilities, such as:
- Does sand erode as easily as gravel?
- How does the rate of water flow affect erosion?
- Will the slope of the table affect erosion?

As the students pose questions, Ms. Cantata writes them on a chart and asks the students to suggest ways they could answer them using the stream table or their models. As the students design their investigations, Ms. Cantata facilitates their thinking with questions such as:
- Which factors will you vary in your study? Which will you keep the same?
- How can you be sure that the rate of water flow is even and constant?
- How will you measure erosion?
- How might varying more than one factor affect your conclusions?

Before the groups proceed with their investigations using the small stream table or their table models, Ms. Cantata reviews their plans. If a group's design is not appropriate, she encourages the students to re-think it. Eventually, all of the groups come up with workable designs.

After several days, when the data have been collected and analyzed, the students report their results. Ms. Cantata encourages them to use visual aids to support their analyses. One group videotapes the erosion under study.

PROGRAMS FOR ELEMENTARY SCIENCE

PRIMARY ELEMENTARY - GRADES K-2

Properties of earth materials

Full Option Science System (FOSS)
Pebbles, Sand, and Silt Module
Introduces primary-level students to basic observable/measurable properties of Earth materials.

Science and Technology for Children (STC)
Soil Unit
Introduces students to the properties of soils and the importance of soil to plant growth.

Changes in the earth and sky

Full Option Science System (FOSS)
Air and Weather Module
Introduces students to weather characteristics and some aspects related to changes of state.

Science and Technology for Children (STC)
Weather Unit
Students are introduced to weather phenomena and how they affect their everyday lives.

MIDDLE ELEMENTARY - GRADES 3-4

Properties of earth materials

Full Option Science System (FOSS)
Earth Materials Module
Introduces students to the concepts of rocks and minerals. Composition and de composition and simple tests are introduced.

Science and Technology for Children (STC)
Rocks and Minerals Unit
Students make observations and descriptions of rocks, noticing similarities and differences.

UPPER ELEMENTARY - GRADES 5-6

Structure of the earth's system

Full Option Science System (FOSS)
Landforms Module
Introduces students to erosion and deposition. Includes 3-D forms, topographic map making and interpretation.

Great Explorations in Math and Science (GEMS)
River Cutters Unit
The concepts of erosion, pollution, and human manipulation of rivers are introduced.

Earth and the solar system

Great Explorations in Math and Science (GEMS)
Earth, Moon, and Stars Unit
Students learn astronomy through the study of the Earth, moon, and stars.

See appendix D for addresses

OTHER TOPICS COVERED BY STANDARD D
Changes in Earth and sky for levels K-4, and *Earth's history* and *Earth in the solar system* for levels 5-8 have not been illustrated. The following resources contain information and activities that cover these topics.

Topic: the planets
Go to: http://www.scilinks.org/
Code: PAE09

Topic: Earth's structure
Go to: http://www.scilinks.org/
Code: PAE010

RESOURCES FOR THE ROAD

Banks, Dale A. (1994, January). Earth, Sun, and Moon: A Moving Experience. *Science Scope, 17* (4), 36-41.

Bellipanni, Lawrence J., and Hazen, Neal. (1994, February). A Wave Tank for Elementary Science. *Science and Children, 31* (5), 23-25.

Brendzel, Sharon. (1994, April). Schoolyard Erosion and Terrain Studies. *Science Scope, 17* (7), 36-38.

Czerniak, Charlene M. (1993, October). The Jurassic Spark. *Science and Children, 31* (2), 19-22.

Fowler, Betty. (1994, September). More "Space" in the Classroom. *Science and Children, 32* (1), 40-41, 55.

Hewitt, Patricia, and Odell, Michael, and Worch, Eric. (1995, November/December). Models Make it Better. *Science Scope, 19* (3), 26-29.

Lowder, Connie C. (1993, November/December). Spelunking in the Classroom. *Science and Children, 31* (3), 19-22.

Mayshark, Robin. (1992, September). Groundwater in a Fish Tank. *Science Scope, 16* (1), 50-52.

Moore, G. Robert. (1994, November/December). Revisiting Science Concepts. *Science and Children, 32* (3), 31-32, 60.

Pinkham, Chester A., and Barrett, Kristin Burrows. (1992, September). Measuring Relative Humidity. *Science and Children, 30* (1), 23-27.

Seagar, Douglas B. (1993, November/December). Where in the World? *Science Scope, 17* (3), 14-18.

Whitney, David E. (1995, February). The Case of the Misplaced Planets. *Science and Children, 32* (5), 12-14, 46.

Wright, Rita F. (1993, January). How High Is Your House? *Science Scope, 16* (4), 16-19.

The full text to most of these resources is available on NSTA's supplementary *Resources for the Road CD-ROM.*

DE RE METALLICA GEORGIUS AGRICOLA

SCIENCE AND TECHNOLOGY

INTRODUCTION

K-6

Children are naturally interested in the human-made (designed) objects such as toys, buildings, automobiles, bridges, can openers or door knobs. Designed objects and materials are an essential element of a child's environment. Ask students to identify designed objects and their uses. This is a good introduction to technology.

The study of familiar, designed objects offers students the chance to apply and improve their observation and problem-solving skills, especially if the objects come from home or school, or some other part of the students' immediate world. We should include a variety of common products and materials, such as clothing, food, vehicles, and computer parts.

The technological design process in some ways resembles scientific inquiry. It involves a five-stage approach that parallels inquiry and includes problem-solving and creative design. Although the stages are modified in the Standards for the upper levels, the general sequence remains the same:
- state the problem
- design an approach
- implement a solution
- evaluate the solution
- communicate the problem, the design, and the solution.

As with the CONTENT STANDARD A (Science as Inquiry), not every activity will involve all five stages.

As children move up through the grades, exploring and improving designs becomes more important. By the end of the K-6 curriculum, building on their earlier design experiences, students will be able to explore the value of using scientific inquiry to produce effective designs.

At the elementary level, technologic design stimulates and engages children in a variety of critical thinking skills. From comparing and contrasting to judging a product's worth, the process helps students make the leap from concrete to abstract.

At the upper elementary level, we might ask students to determine, through observation, the function of a device and the problem that the device was designed to solve. Or we might give students a specific problem and ask them to design a solution—for example, construct a spherical object using only two-dimensional materials and tape or glue. These experiences reinforce the understanding of the relationship between science and technology. Good communication is essential throughout this process.

CONTENT STANDARD E

E

K-4
* As a result of activities in grades K-4, all students should develop
- **Abilities of technological design**
- Understanding about science and technology
- Abilities to distinguish between natural objects and objects made by humans

5-8
As a result of activities in grades 5-8, all students should develop
- Abilities of technological design
- **Understandings about science and technology**

* Bolded statements are discussed in the text

Reprinted with permission from the *National Science Education Standards.* ©1996 National Academy of Sciences. Courtesy of the National Academy Press, Washington, D.C.

SCIENCE AND TECHNOLOGY

CONTENT STANDARD E   K-4

Abilities to distinguish between natural objects and objects made by humans

Nature of the Learner

Students at this level begin to compare objects using multiple characteristics (one at a time). They can place objects in order, and group objects on the basis of similarities or differences.

Get Ready for Science

Objects can be categorized as either natural or designed (human-made). Rocks, trees, and caves are natural, while buildings, bridges, and automobiles are human-made. Students are able to see connections between need, natural resources, technology, and the development of human-made objects.

Wool, sand, and wood are natural, while plastics and metal alloys are considered human-made. The distinction, however, is less obvious for some materials. For example, gasoline occurs naturally but must be extracted, collected, and refined, using technology. Most paper comes from natural sources but has been processed. Some synthetics such as polyester and acrylic are confusing to young students because they resemble natural materials.

Get Set for Instruction

We can help students learn about natural and human-made objects through a variety of instructional and hands-on experiences.

- Students observe objects and materials critically. The characteristics of these items are used to develop an appropriate classification scheme to distinguish between natural and human-made items.
- Students observe familiar urban and rural environments illustrated in slides, overheads, videos, and other multimedia materials. Encourage students to list a variety of natural and human-made objects observed in illustrations.
- Students brainstorm, and make a list of products or materials that would improve student, family, or community life. Challenge student groups to describe the objects, materials, tools, or machines, that they have brainstormed and to identify the natural and human-made materials from which they might be made.
- Students examine designed objects and describe their components.

Assessment

The following activities are will help assess how well students recognize similarities and differences:

- Have students examine designed objects and note if any natural materials were used to make them.
- Give students a variety of human-made and natural objects that they have not studied before. Ask them to sort the objects similarities and differences. Determine the range of characteristics that the students use. Have students group objects into human-made the natural categories.
- Present the students with 10 different items, and ask each student to identify a sorting characteristic and to use it to separate the objects into two groups. Students should then split the groups into subgroups using a different characteristic. When the activity is complete, students should draw a diagram of their grouping scheme.

Primary Elementary, Grades K-2

SCIENCE AND TECHNOLOGY

CONTENT STANDARD E   K-4

Abilities to distinguish between natural objects and objects made by humans

Go! An Example of a Classroom in Action

In Juan Diaz's class, the children have been assembling a collection of natural and human-made objects, including fabrics, plastics, paper products, ceramic objects, metal objects, wood, stones, clay, and various materials used in construction. The students have been encouraged to collect as many different types of materials as possible.

Once the collection is assembled, they examine and study each object, using hand lenses to improve their observations.

Mr. Diaz has also provided a variety of tools to help his students explore the properties of the objects. He has also provided magnets, and small containers filled with water to evaluate whether the objects float or sink.

After the students have completed their observations, Mr. Diaz asks them to divide the objects into two groups. Then he asks them to divide the objects into two groups in a different way. Finally, he asks them to put the objects that are natural in one group

and those that are human-made in the other.

Questions he asks during the course of the lesson:
- Is this object magnetic? Does it dissolve? Does it sink? Does it float?
- What properties did you use to separate the objects into different groups?
- Which of these objects are natural? How can you tell?
- How can you decide if an object is human-made?
- What tools did you use to improve your observations?

━━ Primary Elementary, Grades K-2 ━━

Nature of the Learner

Students at this level continue to improve their ability to design and conduct investigations, analyze results, and communicate the results to others. They begin to organize objects on the basis of multiple properties (one at a time).

Preparing for Science

Science is applied to real-world problems through technological design. By studying design, we gain an understanding of how technological objects and systems work and we gain insight into the laws of nature.

In general, this design process can be broken down into five steps:

- *Identifying the problem:* students learn how to discuss a problem and identify specific tasks related to solving that problem.
- *Designing a solution:* students must examine their proposed solutions critically. Is the solution too expensive or otherwise impractical to construct?
- *Implementation:* involves problem solving and the ability to work with different tools, both individually and collaboratively.
- *Critical examination:* Did the solution work? Could the design be improved? How would you improve it?

A dynamic feedback loop drives the development of a better solution.

- *Communication:* discussing the design steps and other possible solutions.

Nature of Instruction

One of the most effective methods we can use to help children learn about technology design is to have them take part in the experience. By establishing an operational definition, students construct their own knowledge of this essential process.

The design experience may take the form of a classroom challenge in which students could

- develop a better bubble-making solution using detergent, glycerin, water, and different kinds of tools for the bubbles
- create a soft-landing model using parachutes, balloons, or spring shock absorbers
- design a common object using alternate materials (for example, a paper clip composed of toothpicks and rubber bands)

Other instructional strategies to use include
- brainstorming common problems
- taking apart human-made objects, evaluating their design, and investigating alternate designs

Assessment

The design challenge is an excellent assessment tool. Assess students on how well their bubble machine performs, how well they communicate the process and work a cooperatively.

Some activities can be extended as follows:

- Students create a magazine ad that announces the success of their design. It should contain information about the problem, describe the development and implementation of the solution, and present an "unbiased" evaluation.
- Students produce an audio or video recording that communicates the steps of the design process.

In addition, we may also assess students without using an operational definition in the following ways:

- Give students a variety of designed items, such as zippers, batteries, and thermometers. Have them identify the problem these designs solved. Students should explain the human impact of these items and suggest ways they might be improved.
- Show students some ideas for new designs and ask them to describe how each design can be implemented, evaluated, and updated as needed.

🏃 An Example of a Classroom in Action

Helene Citron stages a hands-on challenge each month during the school year. At the beginning of the year, she placed her students in cooperative learning teams. The team members' roles are rotated with each contest.

Now, Ms. Citron's challenge involves constructing a straw-and-clay tower. Any student group that constructs a tower over four feet tall is a winner. If the tower supports a tennis ball for 10 seconds, the group is a super winner.

The materials manager of each group takes 50 straws and a small block of clay. With these each group explores how best to construct the tower. As they build, they evaluate and improve their design.

Ms. Citron reminds the students that all the groups can win any challenge; they are not competing against each other. Even if they do not meet the goal, a group can still win, being evaluated primarily on how well they communicate the steps of their technological de-

sign. Their assessment will also be based on social interaction and cooperation.

During the challenge, Ms. Citron guides her groups with questions such as:
• Have you noticed any patterns on steel bridges?
• Is it good to use a lot of clay to join the straws?
• If you make a square platform as part of the tower, how will you try to hold it up?
• How well did the group work together?

Nature of the Learner

At the upper elementary level, most students recognize logical sequences and organize objects based on several characteristics. They are less egocentric, and are interested in the activities of other people.

Preparing for Science

Science is a way of thinking that addresses the natural world in a manner that is logical, dynamic, and inquiry-based. The foundation of science is observation. To extend our data-gathering ability, we often use tools such as microscopes and telescopes. These devices, allowing us to gain additional information about the natural world.

Technology is the application of science to solving practical problems, doing something more efficiently, or improving the quality of life. Technology increases the ability of humans to overcome their limitations. Designs are created in response to need.

Women and men of all ages and cultural and ethnic backgrounds engage in scientific work. Often, people work together on scientific or technological projects as a team. This cooperative structure relies on individuals, with their own strengths and interests, working together towards a common goal and sharing in the responsibilities and the rewards of the task.

Nature of Instruction

At the upper elementary level the projects are more sophisticated and there is an increased emphasis on team members working cooperatively toward a common goal.

Here are some instructional and hands-on approaches for students:

- Have students study historic breakthroughs in technology and science. They can collect information on the development of tools or techniques such as the electron microscope, polio immunization, or the exploration of distant planets. The research reports should describe how different groups complemented (and sometimes duplicated) each other's research before attaining the goal.

Assessment

We can evaluate student understanding about the nature of science and technology through such alternative assessment activities such as written, oral, and visual presentations problem-solving teams. Other ideas include the following:

- Have students write a scenario that addresses a problem which can be either real or fictitious. Team members should be described in terms of their strengths, weaknesses, background, and interests. The scenario should include the five steps of technological design.
- Have students describe the research by team of scientists or engineers team and how they worked together toward a common goal.

An Example of a Classroom in Action

Michael Stefano enjoys integrating art and science. He often uses role-playing to motivate students and guide their experience with content.

Today's lesson is about the roles of individuals on a technological team. Mr. Stefano explains to his class that each member of the team has specific responsibilities. To demonstrate this, Mr. Stefano has rearranged the chairs and tables in his classroom to represent the Space Shuttle. He has added visuals to the room that suggest Space Shuttle and mission-control environments.

After assigning each student a role as an astronaut or in mission control, Mr. Stefano hands out booklets that contain scripted responses. Then he talks the class through a mock mission.

Weather Officer: *"We have transmitted our latest satellite weather map to you. Do you have a copy of it?"*

Shuttle Pilot: *"Affirmative. We have the weather map."*

Weather Officer: *"Please note that the map indicates a low-pressure region sweeping toward Florida. As you know, low pressure can bring unsettling weather. Therefore, we have decided to change your landing site from Florida to California."*

Shuttle Pilot: *"We copy. We'll have to start reprogramming our computers."*

Medical Officer: *"Attention, mission specialists. We need the data on your pulse rates. Please begin measuring your pulse rate on my mark. I'll stop you after 15 seconds. From the data you gather, you'll have to calculate your pulse in beats per minute."*

Mission Specialist: *"Roger."*

Medical Officer: *"5-4-3-2-1— begin pulse count."*

When the countdown is reached, Mr. Stefano shows the students the videotape *The Dream Is Alive.*

PROGRAMS FOR ELEMENTARY SCIENCE PROGRAMS

PRIMARY ELEMENTARY - GRADES K-2

Abilities To distinguish between natural objects and objects made by humans

Full Option Science System (FOSS)
Wood, Paper, Fabric Modules
These modules introduce students to the properties of natural and human-made objects.

Abilities of technological design

Science for Life and Living (BSCS)
Tools and Machines Unit
Students learn to use simple tools and machines safely and correctly as they complete simple projects.

Science for Life and Living (BSCS)
Materials and Structures Unit
Students learn about structures, then select and arrange the best materials for making the structures.

MIDDLE ELEMENTARY - GRADES 3-4

Abilities of technological design

Full Option Science System (FOSS)
Ideas and Inventions Module
Students use unusual tools for discovering patterns (e.g., chromatography, rubbings, mirror images, and carbon transfers).

Science for Life and Living (BSCS)
Construction and Testing Unit
Students join materials together to strengthen a structure, then change the shape to improve the strength.

Science for Life and Living (BSCS)
Problems and Solutions Unit
Students use the five stages of technological design, and decide whether to change a proposed solution.

UPPER ELEMENTARY - GRADES 5-6

Understanding about science and technology

Science for Life and Living (BSCS)
Constraints and Trade-Offs Unit
Students practice making decisions about real-life problems.

Abilities of technological design

Full Option Science System (FOSS)
Models and Designs Module
Students explore a variety of design problems and work toward improvements of them over time.

Science for Life and Living (BSCS)
Design and Efficiency Unit
Students combine their knowledge of energy and the design process to create energy-efficient devices.

See appendix D for addresses.

OTHER TOPICS COVERED BY STANDARD E

Understandings about science and technology for levels K-4 and *Abilities of technological design* for levels 5-8 have not been illustrated. The following resources contain information and activities that cover these topics.

Topic: microscopes
Go to: http://www.scilinks.org/
Code: PAE11

RESOURCES FOR THE ROAD

The Dream Is Alive (37 min.) (1985). Smithsonian Institution/Lockheed Corporation. Distributed by IMAX Corporation, 3003 Exposition Blvd., Santa Monica, CA 90404. 1-800-263-IMAX, http://www.imax.com/

Cox, Jim. (1994, January). Rube Goldberg Contraptions. *Science Scope*, 17 (4), 44-47.

Etchison, Cindy. (1995, April). Tales from a Technology Teacher. *Science and Children*, 3 (7), 19-21, 30.

Mechling, Kenneth. (1991, February). Consumer Cohorts. *Science Scope*, 14 (5), 20-23.

The full text to most of these resources is available on NSTA's supplementary *Resources for the Road CD-ROM*.

Scientific discoveries, technological innovations, and medical advances promise to make our lives better. They also bring resource shortages, pollution, and other problems. Most of us share a vision of a better future, but projections of global trends, particularly those related to population growth, use of resources, and environmental deterioration, are not encouraging. The effects of these trends will be of increasing concern in the next decades.

Ideas related to health, populations, resources, and the environment prepare students for understanding science-related issues in grades 5 and 6, when students are ready to make the necessary connections between these topics. We can also give our elementary students opportunities to engage in some personal action in local challenges related to science and technology.

By testing ideas against experience and modifying or accepting them in the light of an investigation, elementary students master the concepts and skills that help them understand science-related issues. Whether students modify, accept, or reject an idea depends on how it relates to their experience. We can help elementary students learn to apply science to personal and social perspectives, learn critical thinking and develop the ability to produce useful ideas.

Problems associated with topics in this Standard—personal health, populations, environments, resources, and technology—can be extremely complex because reality is not simple, and it may be hard for students to see the underlying ideas. There is always the question of how much we should simplify problems for students. There is no one solution to this dilemma. In some cases it may be better to accept the complexity of the problem, and in other cases it might be better to break the problem down into simpler components. Our decisions may become easier if we remember that the students' ideas will not remain with them forever. In any case, some students will tackle ideas about the world that we, as teachers, consider too complex for them.

In elementary science programs we extend the perceptions of students from the present to the future, from self to community to society, and from isolated phenomena to interacting systems. Promoting science and technology skills and knowledge will facilitate students' future development as scientifically and technologically literate citizens who will protect the environment, conserve natural resources, and develop greater social harmony in the community and the world.

CONTENT STANDARD F

K-4
* As a result of activities in grades K-4, all students should develop understanding of
- **Personal health**
- Characteristics and changes in populations
- Types of resources
- Changes in environments
- Science and technology in local challenges

5-8
As a result of activities in grades 5-8, all students should develop understanding of
- **Personal health**
- **Populations, resources, and environments**
- Natural hazards
- Risks and benefits
- **Science and technology in society**

* Bolded statements are discussed in the text

Reprinted with persmission from the *National Science Education Standards.* ©1996 National Academy of Sciences. Courtesy of the National Academy Press, Washington, D.C.

Nature of the Learner

Young children expect adults to remove danger and risk from their environment and to provide security. They have a rather vague understanding of safety rules and why they should be followed, but they tend only to understand the consequences of not following them.

They continue to develop connections between action (not wearing a coat) and outcome (catching cold), but they don't consider the intervening variables (lowering resistance).

At the primary elementary level, most students

- use the term "germs" for all microbes
- tentatively connect eating certain foods with being healthy
- understand environmental hazards (such as pollution) only to the extent that they themselves might be affected in some direct way

 **Get Ready for Science**

Good health requires important habits and behaviors that contribute to our individual welfare. Students develop an understanding that cleanliness, nutrition, exercise, and rest are necessary for good health.

Safety means freedom from danger. It is a basic human need. The desire to feel safe is closely aligned with developing confidence and avoiding anxiety and fear. Our primary concern is our own physical well-being. It is vital that we develop a set of rules to keep our bodies safe and healthy.

From an early age, children need to follow rules and make logical decisions (such as to look both ways before crossing the street) for their own safety and health.

Get Set for Instruction

Students learn to make wise decisions about safety by processing their own and others' decisions. They can learn this in a variety of ways and situations, such as

- being briefed for field trips
- examining automobile traffic patterns around the school
- discussing incidents from the newspaper

Students discuss specific safety-related situations in pairs ("What would you do?") and then share their conclusions with the class. We should consider students' feelings as well as their decisions when dealing with safety, security, and risk.

Assessment

Continuous monitoring of students, with particular attention to their behavior and conversations, is one of the most effective assessment tools. Here is a specific example:

- Choose a situation in which students are involved in deciding safety on school grounds. Arrange the students in pairs to discuss the pros and cons of various alternatives. Listen to the discussions and write down the key ideas, comments, and thoughts of each student. Later, analyze the notes, and date and file them by topic.

Primary Elementary, Grades K-2

Go!
An Example of a
Classroom in Action

Barbara Daly has asked her students to draw a story line about a day in their lives. The students have written or illustrated the events in chronological order, from the time they woke up in the morning to when they went to sleep at night.

Ms. Daly looks for opportunities to have her students think about the health and safety aspects of their day. For example, she asks:

- Did you brush your teeth after meals? How often should teeth be brushed? What does brushing accomplish?
- When did you wash your hands?

- What about bathing or showering? When is this important, and why?

Ms. Daly is careful not to embarrass children who might not have good health habits. The class discusses these subjects in general ways that are helpful to all students. Specific ideas are discussed concerning common events such as how to care for a cut or bruise.

The class explores safety ideas in response to the parts of the stories in which the children were going from one place to another or were engaged in active games. Ms. Daly asks what the students remember about safety while traveling.

- What does a stop sign or a red traffic signal mean?
- What should you do when crossing a street?
- What should you do if someone you don't know offers you a ride?

Ms. Daly considers it important for young children to learn to be thoughtful about personal health and safety. She finds it effective to have her students recall the times in their daily lives when they should apply these ideas. And she believes that discussing these topics from time to time in different contexts promotes her students' welfare.

Primary Elementary, Grades K-2

Nature of the Learner

Middle elementary level students are beginning to develop an interest in how their bodies work. Because some students have experienced broken bones and all of them have been sick, they bring a variety of personal experiences to the study of their bodies.

Preparing for Science

Humans take their physical shape from the basic framework called the *skeleton*. The sheer number of bones of different shapes, sizes, and purposes is difficult to imagine. Bones don't move themselves, but must be pulled by a source of power. *Muscles* provide that power and *tendons* connect muscles to the bones. Muscles have the ability to contract, or shorten, on demand; when they do, the bones move. Muscles always pull on bones.

The human body requires *food* to carry out its functions. The *nutritional values* of various foods help us determine whether or not a particular food will contribute to our health. Foods are often combinations of different nutrients. Recommendations for good nutrition include not eating too much fat and sugar.

Nature of Instruction

Students learn about personal health by studying the structures of the human body, and the functions of these structures, and nutrition as the source of energy.

Here are some examples:
- Have students rub small, equal-sized samples of several different foods like butter, potato chips, peanut butter, and candy, on paper towels. Let the towels sit for several hours. Then measure the size of the spots left by the foods to determine which foods had the most fat in them.
- Using their classmates as models, have children build a rough model of the skeletal system.

The experiences we provide should be firsthand and personal, so that students are free to develop their own ideas,

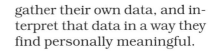

gather their own data, and interpret that data in a way they find personally meaningful.

We can enhance learning by using inquiry strategies—asking questions, structuring cooperative groups, monitoring for assessment, extending the scope of the activities, and providing class time and needed materials.

Assessment

Monitoring students as they work in groups is a very effective way of gathering information about what our students know and can do. Listen to students' ideas and observe how they approach the task at hand. Both systematic and anecdotal assessment schemes work well in this situation. For example:
- To assess how well students understand bones and their function, give them a mystery bone made of plaster and ask them to identify what part of the animal it came from and what function it performed.
- To assess how well students apply a procedure to new food substances, give them several foods that they have not studied and ask them to determine which contains the most and the least fat. Students should design a way to find out the fat content of each and then use the results to place the foods in order, from most to least fatty.

Middle Elementary, Grades 3-4

An Example of a Classroom in Action

Working in pairs, the students in Mr. Brickman's class have traced each others hands on sheets of paper. They are now deciding where to draw the bones, how many bones there are, and the size of each by feeling their own hands and talking to each other. When they are finished, they will hang their drawings on the wall for all to examine, compare, and discuss.

On another day, Mr. Brickman will bring X-rays of human hands for the students to study. The students will then have the opportunity to modify their original drawings.

While the students are drawing and discussing the bones in their hands, Mr. Brickman is roaming the room listening in on conversations, occasionally jotting down an overheard conversation or making notes on an observed behavior.

Once in a while, he will ask a question such as:
• Do you think you each have a different number of bones in your hands? Would both of your hands have the same number of bones? How could you find out?
• What must the joints look like in order to allow your hand to bend?
• Do adults have more, fewer, or the same number of bones as you?
• If you could see inside your hand, how many joints would it have?
• How many bones do you think there are in your body? How could you find out?

Nature of the Learner

Upper elementary students have learned a great deal about safety, but are still prone to respond to peer pressure and disregard their own common sense.

Most students understand the relationship between diet, exercise, and health.

 ## Preparing for Science

It is important for students to recognize the potential for accidents and the existence of hazards. Safe living requires taking precautions and recognizing risks when making decisions. Injury prevention has both personal and social dimensions.

We can control many factors related to health, such as personal health habits, diet, exercise, and avoidance of substance abuse. Regular exercise is important for good health and can improve mental health.

Illness is caused by various factors, including environmental conditions. Natural environments may contain substances that are harmful to humans. Technology and population growth can cause pollution. Maintaining environmental health involves establishing quality standards and monitoring procedures

Nature of Instruction

Upper elementary students are beginning to show interest in issues of health and safety. Laboratory activities on environment-related issues are most meaningful when augmented by surveys and critical readings.

The following are some examples of appropriate activities we might use concerning safety and security:

- Draw a map of the school and its grounds; then identify and plot locations where accidents tend to occur (bicycle racks, stairways, athletic fields, doorways, and school sidewalks).
- Conduct a survey to find out if boys or girls have more accidents.
- Conduct research to find out the types of accidents

that occur most frequently around the school and construct a bar graph to show these data.

Assessment

We might use some of the following opportunities for assessing every student's spacing understanding of health and safety:

- Note incidents in which students look out for themselves or their neighbors.
- Have students design and conduct an assessment in which they determine the general state of their own health.
- Design a task and use a checklist to assess students' proficiency in developing skills required for performing classroom and playground activities.
- Have students create and display posters illustrating various safety precautions that should be taken around the school.

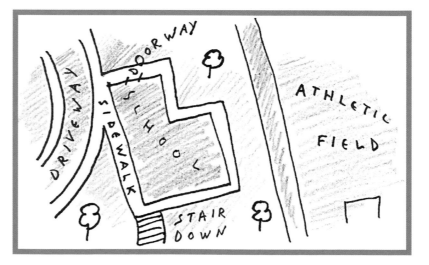

An Example of a Classroom in Action

Joe Ponzio has set up a series of activities so that his students can study the social dynamics of their school population. For several weeks, the students have been working on two projects.

First, the class surveyed the school's students to find out how they travel to and from school. When the class finished interpreting their data, they raised some questions for discussion:
• Which are the most efficient way by which students go to and from school?
• If every student were transported in a car, what effects would the increased traffic have on the area around the school?

When the students expressed concern about several issues—congestion, safety problems, noise, and air and water pollution—Mr. Ponzio challenged them to design a plan to improve or eliminate the conditions.

Next, the students made maps of "people paths"—places on the school grounds where students and teachers travel or congregate at different times of the day. Analysis of the data focused on such questions as
• Are some places more crowded than others?
• Do girls and boys tend to frequent different pathways?
• Is the school designed in a way that facilitates or hinders the interaction of students and adults outside of the classroom?

Mr. Ponzio asked his students to make recommendations that would promote the personal safety, comfort, and welfare of all individuals on the school grounds. The students identified and assessed risks and reviewed school rules, such as "Don't run in the hallways", which are designed to protect students and others from accidents and hazards. They evaluated the rules, made suggestions for improving them, and drew up some new ones that they felt were necessary. Then they communicated their recommendations to the rest of the school.

Nature of the Learner

Upper elementary students continue to improve their ability to record, synthesize, and interpret data independently. They begin to determine what data is needed to solve a problem and to recognize the relationship between explanation and evidence.

Preparing for Science

A **resource** can be defined as something needed by an organism, a population, or an ecosystem for survival. Some resources are air, water, food, sunlight, and soil. Humans rely on many resources for materials, energy, and the production of food. The following diagram illustrates one way to group these types of resources:

All of the non-living resources that we will ever have on Earth are already here (except for the occasional meteorite). As we continue to use up Earth's resources, we will find it more difficult and more costly to obtain new raw ma-

terials. **Recycling** is the process of recovering used materials. Resources will last longer if we recycle them. Recycling treats the symptoms (litter and depletion of resources) rather than the illness caused by wasteful habits, overconsumption, and carelessness).

Supply and demand as it relates to consuming resources is simple: prices fall when supplies are abundant and rise when supplies are limited. Many resources cannot be obtained at reasonable costs, and so are not available for human use. However, new discoveries, improved technology, and higher prices can make the mining or harvesting of resources cost effective. Many resources are increased through reuse, conservation, and substitution.

The following are some issues that relate to the use and conservation of Earth's resources:
- What are some of the major costs of producing materials?

- Show the environmental impact of mining, processing, and producing metals

Nature of Instruction

Students gain an understanding of resources and related issues through a variety of experiences, such as
- monitoring the amount of paper used and wasted in their class during a week, then brainstorming ways to conserve paper in school
- developing strategies for recycling some paper from their classes
- exploring the natural resources used in producing a product
- playing a game in which the students decide on the amount of a resource they would like, then keep track of the its use in order to understand supply and demand
- playing a game about the distribution of resources, then following up with group decision-making on the distribution of resources

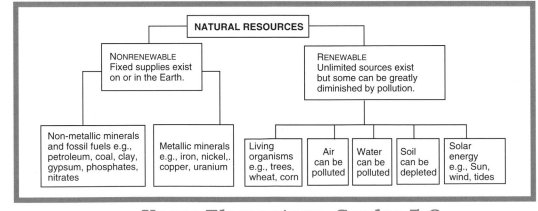

Diagram:

NATURAL RESOURCES

NONRENEWABLE — Fixed supplies exist on or in the Earth.

RENEWABLE — Unlimited sources exist but some can be greatly diminished by pollution.

- Non-metallic minerals and fossil fuels e.g., petroleum, coal, clay, gypsum, phosphates, nitrates
- Metallic minerals e.g., iron, nickel,. copper, uranium
- Living organisms e.g., trees, wheat, corn
- Air can be polluted
- Water can be polluted
- Soil can be depleted
- Solar energy e.g., Sun, wind, tides

Upper Elementary, Grades 5-6

Assessment

An assessment in which students keep a journal about the concept of resources would indicate their attitudes and feelings toward issues associated with this subject, including:
- a study of resources used by students at home and at school
- a description of the difference between reserves and resources
- an explanation of the roles of technology and economics in extracting resources
- why decisions concerning Earth's resources are complex
- a description of the environmental consequences of extracting resources.

An Example of a Classroom in Action

Al Balmer wants his sixth grade students to discover the difference between material reserves and resources. Before his students arrive at school, he distributes 200 pennies around the classroom. 50 of them are visible and easy to reach, 150 are out of sight or in places that are difficult to reach. He sets out tweezers, toothpicks, and mirrors for later use. He tells his students that the pennies, representing natural resources, are located around the room. He explains that each penny represents a source of copper that could become a copper mine. He divides his students into groups of four and assigns sections of the room to each group.

The students are given 5 minutes to look around the room to determine approximately how many pennies they can see and note their locations. Al Balmer tells the students they must not collect any pennies during this part of the activity.

Then he calls his asks each group to report on the number of pennies located (copper reserves). He lists these on the chalkboard and asks if there might be other pennies (copper resources) that have not been located. He puts the following definitions on the board for discussion:

Reserves: The amount of an Earth material in known locations.
Resources: The total amount of an Earth material.

Students estimate the size of the copper resources in the classroom and record their estimates on the board. Then, for 15 minutes, they "mine" the reserves (the located pennies) using only the "technology" of tweezers, toothpicks, and mirrors and keeping track of the number of pennies they "extract" each minute of mining.

When "time" is called, students graph the number of pennies found each minute. The students find that there is a steady decrease in the pennies found per minute.

Questions that Mr. Balmer might ask during this experience include:
- How did the use of technology (mirrors, tweezers, and toothpicks) help?
- What happened as the extraction of pennies continued over time?
- How close were your estimates of the resource?
- Are there more resources? How do you know? How many more?
- What would be the environmental consequences of moving furniture?
- What problems did you experience after more time elapsed?

Nature of the Learner

Most upper elementary students continue to improve their ability to organize ideas, and to observe, measure, record, synthesize, and interpret data. They begin to recognize the relationship between explanation and evidence.

Preparing for Science

Science has improved our lives in many ways, the most obviously in the field of medicine. Since the beginning of this century, the human life span has been increased by decades, thanks to the discovery of medications like antibiotics and vaccines and improved surgical skills.

The effect of science on society is neither entirely beneficial nor entirely detrimental. Science has sometimes led some people to draw conclusions that are disturbing and has fostered some technologies that have been ecologically disastrous.

Some people blame science for having a detrimental effect on society, and want scientists to pursue only research that will not conflict with our values or result in environmental degradation. Science, however, is neutral. It looks at natural phenomena in order to understand them

better. Business, society, and economics influence how science is used. Thus, we are all responsible for influencing the forces that determine how to use scientific knowledge for the benefits of living organisms.

Nature of Instruction

Students explore science and technology in society through experiences such as

- investigating whether a plant fertilized with synthetic chemical fertilizer grows as well as or better than one fertilized with natural plant and animal material
- debating what responsibility scientists have for anticipating the effects of their work on society
- listing what actions *are* taking place and what actions *should be* taking place for determining
  a) the effects on the atmosphere of carbon dioxide from automobiles, power plants, and factories

b) the effects on humans of drugs and chemicals of all kinds

c) the long-term consequences of our destruction of plants, animal species, forests, plains, and oceans.

Assessment

An assessment in which students keep a journal showing what they think about related concepts reveals their attitudes about science and technology in society.

Here are some possible entries we might ask students to include in the journal:

- A list of the pros and cons of different kinds of technology.
- A report on an investigation or a controlled experiment to determine the effects of new technology.
- Newspaper articles about new technology and science discoveries along with a discussion of the possible impacts on the environment.

An Example of a Classroom in Action

Ed Willis tells his class that statistics show that Americans have never been safer. The life expectancy at birth in 1986 was 74.8 years, which was 4 years more than it was in 1970, largely because of a dramatic drop in deaths from heart disease and stroke.

Next, Mr. Willis asks his students if they think the American public should have a say about the use of nuclear power. He provides some data that indicate that only three lives have been claimed in nuclear accidents in the United States in the last 30 years. He notes that many Americans choose not wear seat belts while riding in automobiles, and as a result many people die each year. Students work in groups of four to develop arguments that support or reject various ideas about what to do on these issues.

The next day, Mr. Willis continues the discussion by asking whether people should base decisions about such matters solely on the number of deaths, injuries, and damage at stake. He asks if there are other important feelings and values people need to consider in making decisions about risk. The students discuss these issues in their groups and list other considerations in making a risk decision.

Mr. Willis challenges his students to determine how they might make decisions involving risks to their lives and health when they know some things harm them. Students talk about this issue and share their views with the class.

(for more ideas, see Richard Wilson, 1985.)

PROGRAMS FOR ELEMENTARY SCIENCE

PRIMARY ELEMENTARY - GRADES K-2

Personal health

Science for Life and Living (BSCS)
Safety and Security Unit
Students practice behaviors likely to prevent injuries; and procedures to follow in potentially unsafe situations.

Science for Life and Living (BSCS)
Wellness and Personal Care Unit
Students learn responsibility for their health practice personal care habits to improve their health.

MIDDLE ELEMENTARY - GRADES 3-4

Personal health

Full Option Science System (FOSS)
Human Body Module
Introduces the skeletal and muscular systems of the body, including care and personal health.

Science for Life and Living (BSCS)
Nutrition and Dental Care Unit
Students learn three rules for good nutrition: eat a variety of foods, eat less sugar, eat less fat.

Science for Life and Living (BSCS)
Self and Substances Unit
Students explore how decisions about substance use are influenced by family, peers, and personal values.

UPPER ELEMENTARY - GRADES 5-6

Personal health

Chemical, Health, Environment, and Me (CHEM)
Smoking and My Health Unit
Students use a smoking machine to understand the impact of smoking on health.

Full Option Science System (FOSS)
Food and Nutrition Module
Introduces students to nutrition factors, the effects they have on the human body, ways to test foods.

Great Explorations in Math and Science (GEMS)
Vitamin C Testing Unit
Students perform simple chemical tests to compare the vitamin C content of different foods.

Science and Technology for Children (STC)
Food Chemistry Unit
Introduces students to basic concepts related to food and nutrition through physical and chemical tests.

Science for Life and Living (BSCS)
Fitness and Protection Unit
Students learn about safety procedures and equipment that will protect them from injury.

Populations and resources

Chemical, Health, Environment, and Me (CHEM)
Trash or Cash Unit
Students collect and categorize classroom trash to understand solid waste problems and possible solutions.

Risks and benefits

Chemical, Health, Environment, and Me (CHEM)
The Hazardous Home Unit
Students identify hazardous chemicals in the home and set up a home hazards inventory.

See appendix D for addresses

OTHER TOPICS COVERED BY STANDARD F

Characteristics and changes in populations, Types of resources, Changes in environments, and Science and technology in local challenges for levels K-4, and *Motions and forces* for levels 5-8 have not been illustrated. The following resources contain information and activities that cover these topics.

SCI LINKS
THE WORLD'S A CLICK AWAY

Topic: natural resources
Go to: http://www.scilinks.org/
Code: PAE12

Topic: resource depletion
Go to: http://www.scilinks.org/
Code: PAE13

RESOURCES FOR THE ROAD

Bybee, Rodger; Peterson, Rita; Bowyer, Jane; and Butts, David. (1984). *Teaching About Science and Society: Activities for Elementary and Junior High School.* Columbus, OH: Charles E. Merrill.

Habib, Gary, and Anderson, Kathryn, and Hawkins, Cassandra. (1995, February). Science in the Courtroom: A Healthy Diet on Trial. *Science Scope, 18 (5),* 16-20.

Keller, J. David, and Holden, Pamela. (1994, November/December). Science Guides Consumer Choices. *Science*
and Children, 32 (3), 20-23, 55.

Moseley, Christine. (1995, May). The Continuing Adventures of the Truffala Tree Company. *Science Scope, 18 (6),* 22-25.

Palmer, Jacqueline. (1992, November/December). The Garbage Game. *Science Scope, 16 (3),* 16-22.

Rivera, Deborah, and Banbury, Mary. (1994, May). Conserving Water: Every Drop Makes a Difference. *Science Scope, 17 (8),* 15-19.

Stanley, Lois R. (1995, January). A River Runs Through Science Learning. *Science and Children, 32 (4),* 13-15, 58.

Voorhis, Ken. (1993, November/December). Taking a Course in Nature. *Science and Children, 31 (3),* 23-26.

Wilson, Richard. (1985, October). Staying Alive in the 20th Century, *Science 85,* 31-39.

The full text to most of these resources is available on NSTA's supplementary *Resources for the Road CD-ROM.*

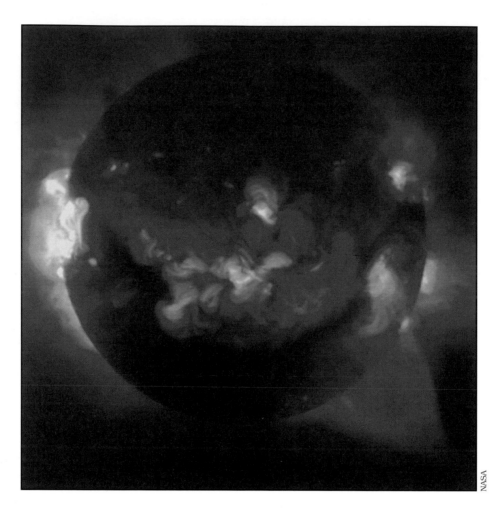

NASA

Throughout history, great scientific discoveries have been made by mavericks who dared to challenge accepted ideas. Studying the lives of scientists like Copernicus, Darwin, and Pasteur helps students see how the attitudes of scientific inquiry exhibited by these great scientists led to discoveries that challenged the accepted ideas of their times.

The common thread of the Standards for the history and nature of science is that science is a human endeavor. Indeed, the study of science is a natural intellectual and social endeavor—an attempt to understand how the world works.

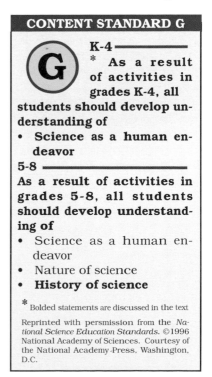

As students develop cognitively through the school years, they become more able to handle complex and abstract explanations about the history and nature of science. Eventually they will be able to develop a scientific world view, become expert at scientific inquiry, and understand the scientific enterprise.

We should give elementary students a variety of opportunities to establish a foundation upon which to build expertise and abstractions. This foundation should include enjoyable hands-on, minds-on experiences with natural and social phenomena. Students need to engage in "doing science," conducting investigations, and explaining their findings. They will draw on these experiences later, when they reflect on the process of science. Historical examples can help younger students learn how scientists work and older students learn how scientific ideas become accepted by the scientific community.

The idea that scientific knowledge is always subject to change may be difficult for students to grasp. We can explain that new questions are constantly asked, new theories are continually being proposed, new instruments are invented, and new techniques are developed for conducting scientific research. However, it is also important to point out that the main body of scientific knowledge is very stable and expands slowly.

Throughout history, great scientific discoveries have been made by mavericks who dared to challenge accepted ideas. Studying the lives of scientists like Copernicus, Darwin, and Pasteur helps students see how the attitudes of scientific inquiry exhibited by these great scientists led to discoveries that challenged the accepted ideas of their times.

Curiosity is the inspiration for doing science. Scientists are question-askers and observations they make can be the catalyst for an investigation. Scientists develop hypotheses, draw inferences from direct observation of natural phenomena, and withhold judgments until all the data have been accumulated. They must be ready to set aside previously held views in light of new information. We should encourage elementary students to ask questions about nature, to count and measure, make qualitative observations and discuss their findings.

CONTENT STANDARD G

G

K-4
* As a result of activities in grades K-4, all students should develop understanding of
- **Science as a human endeavor**

5-8
As a result of activities in grades 5-8, all students should develop understanding of
- Science as a human endeavor
- Nature of science
- **History of science**

* Bolded statements are discussed in the text

Nature of the Learner

Most primary elementary students are naturally curious and ask questions. They are highly egocentric, but they can communicate their observations to others. They can understand stories and are able to tell stories of their own.

 **Get Ready for Science**

Science is a human endeavor. Building on the ideas of the past has established civilizations and has led us to our current level of technology. People in every culture have developed explanations for occurrences in the natural world which have been passed down through history. By asking new questions and inventing new ways to test old explanations, we add new information to our lives.

The gradual evolution of modern science has been the work of many women and men from a variety of backgrounds.

 **Get Set for Instruction**

It is important for us to give our students a variety of opportunities—field studies, kits in and out of the classroom, and hands-on activities—to show them that science is a natural human endeavor.

We should capitalize on our students' curiosity by leading them to ask better questions and to try to find reasonable explanations. We can help them to recognize what is "reasonable" and what is not. We can guide them toward making more sophisticated observations by using more than one sense, then converting their qualitative observations into quantitative ones by using measuring tools.

Assessment

It is better to approach assessing student understanding of the history of science indirectly in the early primary years. At this age, students begin to understand the value of having standard units of measurement, supporting explanations with evidence (data), and communicating information to others. Here are some examples of ways we might test students' grasp of these concepts:

- Ask students to demonstrate ways in which measuring is used in different occupations and to explain why they think it is or is not important to measure with rulers or meter sticks.

- Suppose that two students need the same costumes for a school play. Let students determine how someone can be sure the two costumes look alike.

- Have students make up a story to tell their fellow students explaining where the Sun is at night. Ask them to give evidence supporting the story.

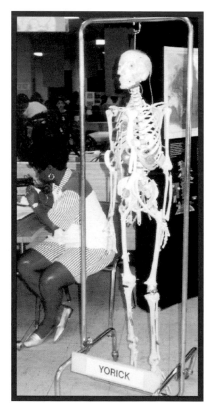

YORICK

Primary Elementary, Grades K-2

Go!
An Example of a
Classroom in Action

While outside at recess, several students heard a strange sound. They alerted their teacher, Jules Smith, and followed the sound to an unusual insect making a chirping sound on the trunk of a tree. Mr. Smith sent a student to get a clear plastic container in which to collect the insect.

Inside the classroom, the students observed the insect, watching its movements and recording its sounds. Mr. Smith enlisted his students' help in generating questions about the insect, so the children decided to find out everything they could about it. Some students looked in books; others interviewed older students and adults; others worked with the art teacher to make models of the insect; and others talked to their parents about how to find a scientist who could visit the class and talk to the students about the insect.

The students compiled their information and are now making drawings. They will go to another classroom, where each will be paired with another student. They will share their insect drawings and tell what they have learned about the insect.

After they release the insect where they found it, Mr. Smith and the students will discuss how they found answers to their questions.

Nature of the Learner

Most middle elementary students understand what people do at work and begin to understand that a career requires serious effort and the application of learning. Students continue to improve their ability to collect and share data.

Preparing for Science

Science is a human endeavor. Occupations involve performing tasks. Students see people questioning, focusing on activities they enjoy, and eventually specializing in an area of interest—an occupation or hobby.

We live in a society quite different from that of our parents and grandparents, and many new inventions and discoveries have improved our lives. But there is much that is still not understood; scientific investigations and discoveries are not over. Many men and women use some science as part of their occupation; others engage in science full-time as a career.

Nature of Instruction

We should encourage student's observations and comparisons. Posing questions, gathering data, and reporting findings are human activities that students are able to understand. We should allow students to work cooperatively and we should encourage individual students to incorporate their observations and ideas into group decisions.

If we provide opportunities for students to use a variety of sources of information about a topic, they will begin to compare the reliability of these sources. This might be accomplished by using simple equipment and tools to gather data and to extend the senses. Calculators and computers can serve as excellent bridges to other technologies. Here are some examples:

- To introduce the idea of the relationship between evidence and explanation, select examples of historical figures and discuss how well their ideas were accepted during their lifetime and afterward.
- Using stories, films, and videos, present examples of the contributions to scientific knowledge made by women and by people from different ethnic and cultural backgrounds.
- Have students investigate various careers in science.
- Investigate evidence for the study of science in early times.

Assessment

At this age, students can support their explanations with more reliable data than in the earlier grades. We can also expect them to make use of technologies that are available to them. In this way, they can become more proficient communicators through the creative use of media. Activities we might find suitable for assessment include the following:

- Have students find photos of a modern kitchen and compare them with illustrations of kitchens from about 1900 to 1920. Let students describe differences in appliances, plumbing, and so on. Ask them to speculate about why these changes occurred and why other changes did not.
- Challenge students to design an investigation to determine the best paper towel. Insist they define "best" (for example, most economical, most absorbent, or strongest).
- Ask students to describe a job that existed in the 1950s and is still being done today. Have them describe how science was and is used in that job and then discuss whether science has changed the job in any way. Assess how well students gather the data they need, organize the data, and present their findings.

An Example of a Classroom in Action

Henry Blanchard wondered if his students could see science at work in the world around them. His students already knew that scientists followed certain procedures to find answers to questions, but Mr. Blanchard wasn't sure the students could apply their skills to everyday situations. He decided to send them on a Science Skills Scavenger Hunt to find the different ways adults use science in their work.

The students spend time preparing for their detective work by reviewing the skills they used when they grew bean plants. They also make a list of people who work in and around their school but who are not teachers. Mr. Blanchard divides the class into groups and helps them design a checklist of skills and questions the "detectives" can ask in their interviews.

After all the students have finished their tasks, each group will make a chart or graph of their checklist information and pick out the best comments from the interviews. Then, one representative from each group will help make a class chart based on all the groups' work. Some students plan to report their findings in the school newsletter, while others will make a bulletin board display for the hall by the office.

Nature of the Learner

Upper elementary level students are learning to solve problems and perform experiments more independently. They ask complex and multi-level questions and use a more formal approach to problem solving. They imagine themselves being in an occupation.

 ### Preparing for Science

Science is a human endeavor. In addition to observing people in various scientific careers, students realize that scientists usually concentrate their research on one particular field of endeavor or interest.

To accomplish goals in science, engineering, and health professions, people sometimes work in teams and sometimes they work alone. Whether working individually or with others, scientists build new information on previous knowledge and communicate their findings in a variety of ways.

Sometimes faulty explanations persist for a long time in a particular cultural context, and it takes new evidence and many years for a new idea to gain acceptance. Eventually, breakthrough ideas are reaffirmed or refuted through additional investigations and experiments. Many women and men throughout history overcame technical, social, and cultural obstacles to communicate innovative information that seems obvious to us today.

Nature of Instruction

Encourage students to work cooperatively, ask questions, brainstorm ideas, and discuss results. Each member of the group should contribute to data collection, data analysis, and the reporting of results.

Continue to emphasize the relationship between evidence and explanation and the role that each has played throughout history.

We need to help students develop the skills they need to evaluate sources of information and the information itself. This aspect of instruction is also desirable for its historical perspective.

Themes that are appropriate for teaching the history of science include
- the impact of inventions and discoveries on various societies and cultures
- historical figures who made significant contributions to scientific knowledge

Assessment

Students should be able to examine and analyze the relationship between culture and the scientific inventions and discoveries made during an historical period. This helps students understand that science builds continuously on previous knowledge and is still evolving.

In each of the following examples, we assess the quality of student arguments: the amount of research used to build a case, the organization of the ideas, and the respect for points of view of others.
- Ask students to compare two sources of information (such as a tabloid and an encyclopedia) on the same topic. Which is more reliable? How can they tell?
- Have students research explorers or traders who traveled great distances across oceans before 1500 AD, and then ask them to explain why some people persisted in believing Earth was flat even until Columbus's voyages in the late 1400s.
- Challenge students to give two examples of proof that Earth is shaped like a sphere and not like a flat table top.
- Ask the students to research the lives of early scientists and explain their contributions to our knowledge.

Upper Elementary, Grades 5-6

CAROL UPCHURCH

An Example of a Classroom in Action

Leonardo da Vinci is said to have been ahead of his time. Sara Milstein wants her students to see that often people's culture, status in society, or the historical period in which they live may prevent the wide acceptance of their new scientific idea or explanation.

She divides her class into groups to study Leonardo da Vinci, Tycho Brahe, Isaac Newton, George Washington Carver, Marie Curie, and Thomas Jefferson. One of the groups wonders why there are so few names of women and people from Asia, Africa, and South America. Some students form groups to look for women scientists and scientists from other cultures.

The school's library and media center is the focus of their research. The students use CD-ROM encyclopedias, information from the Internet, and biographies. The class has decided to create its own cross-referenced database and to add to it throughout the year. At the end of the semester, each student will receive a copy of the class database on a diskette.

As the year progresses, Mrs. Milstein asks students these questions about the scientists they have encountered:
• Did these scientists receive help from other scientists?
• What kind of reaction did the work of the scientists receive from other scientists and nonscientists?

OTHER TOPICS COVERED BY STANDARD G

Science as a human endeavor and *Nature of science* for levels 5-8 have not been illustrated. The following resources and the *Pathways CD-ROM* contain information and activities that cover these topics.

Topic: careers in life science
Go to: http://www.scilinks.org/
Code: PAE14

Topic: careers in Earth science
Go to: http://www.scilinks.org/
Code: PAE15

RESOURCES FOR THE ROAD

Dills, William L. Jr. (1992, November/December). The Great Wintergreen Candy Experiment. *Science Scope, 16* (3), 24-27.

Hampton, Elaine, and Gallegos, Charles. (1994, March). Science for All Students. *Science Scope, 17* (6), 5-8.

Hoofman, Judy. (1994, March). My Summer with Leonardo and Other Wonderful Experiences. *Science and Children, 31* (6), 22-24.

Marcoux, Mary, and Thompson, Sylvia. (1996, February). Colonial Science. *Science and Children, 33* (5), 12-15, 35.

Marturano, Arlene. (1995, February). Horticulture and Human Culture. *Science and Children, 32* (5), 26-29, 50.

McDuffie, Thomas E. Jr., and Smith, Bruce E. (1995, April). Has Anyone Seen the I in Roy G. BIV?, *Science Scope, 18* (7), 30-33.

Project 2061, American Association for the Advancement of Science. (1993). *Benchmarks for Science Literacy.* New York: Oxford University Press.

Rakow, Steven J. (1986). *Teaching Science as Inquiry.* Bloomington, IN: Phi Delta Kappa Educational Foundation.

The full text to most of these resources is available on NSTA's supplementary *Resources for the Road CD-ROM.*

Program Standards

To effect change in programs, we will have to accept positions of leadership in our communities. And to do that, we will have to believe in ourselves.

Moving into the Program Standards

Every child is born a scientist. Children have the nonstop curiosity that prompts them continually to compare their internal world with the input of their senses and struggle to make sense of it all. It is the challenge of elementary science to keep that curiosity alive!

What Makes a Good Science Program?

What does a good science program look like in light of the Standards? The Standards define a good program as one that is designed around student knowledge, skills, and attitudes.

The science program for all students in grades K–6 should include all the Content Standards (see **page 134**) embedded in inquiry-centered curriculum patterns that are developmentally appropriate, interesting, and relevant to students' lives. The science program in every elementary classroom must be an integral part of daily activities and other subjects so that students will know science is an important component of their everyday lives.

Inquiry Is Key

From kindergarten through 12th grade, inquiry is the thread that binds science courses and programs together. Teachers should give all students opportunities to engage in and reflect on natural phenomena through the process of inquiry (searching, organizing, experimenting, and communicating). This is the heart of science. The student who learns how to question, explore, find answers, and solve problems is on the path to the wonderful experience of learning!

The Standards call for aligning good teaching, assessment, and systems support to make high student expectations a reality. They ask program designers to spend time defining student outcomes and to consider how they expect to see (assessment) them when they occur. They ask schools to consider what levels of modification and compensatory education will provide optimal "opportunity to learn" for *all* students. Perhaps most importantly, they ask schools and systems to consider how to support good ideas.

LEEZA GLISSON

The six Program Standards address the following issues:

- consistency in the program: Is the program consistent? Is it paced at a developmentally appropriate rate?
- curriculum: Does the curriculum connect to other areas of learning and to the students' world?
- mathematics in science: Are the necessary mathematical tools embedded in and integrated into the program?
- resources: Is the program supported by the time, space, and equipment that is necessary for student growth at each level?
- equity and excellence: Does the program give diverse learners equal footing?
- schools as communities of learners: Does the faculty and school community support and continually renew the program?

A Consistent Flow

Often the goals of school programs change as students move from grade to grade. Today's elementary science demands informational read-ing, while middle school science builds skills, and secondary science stresses memorization. While individual courses may look coherent, they may be very inconsistent from the perspective of the student.

The Standards challenge school systems to design science programs with consistent goals for student-learning throughout the grade levels. One approach is to emphasize real-world applications and societal implications to tie coursework together across the grades.

Resources and Opportunity To Learn

We cannot define expectations for students without looking at the necessary conditions for realistic "opportunity to learn." Appropriate materials, class size, schedules, storage, and classroom space are all essential for inquiry-based learning. These resources become even more crucial when systems are reaching for equity between students of varied abilities and backgrounds.

The physical environment greatly influences the direction and quality of student experiences in science. Communities that want good science programs must support them with facilities that accommodate active exploration, positive collaboration, and safe investigation. (For more information about setting up facilities for teaching

elementary science, see Appendix C.)

The arrangement of the classroom should be flexible so that it can be changed to accommodate various learning activities. There should be adequate space for groups of students and individuals to work safety. Reference materials should be readily available. These recommendations apply to *every* grade level in the elementary school.

Another factor that affects the design of science classrooms is inclusion. Most students with physical or learning challenges benefit from heterogeneous class experiences in science. To accommodate these students, changes in traditional construction and in instruction have to occur.

Teachers have the responsibility of informing themselves and their students about the potential hazards of exploratory science. All safety rules must be followed at all times. Plugs without ground fault interrupters or cabinets without locks must have attention. Reconfiguring and adding learning space may have to wait until the next round of construction in your district, but safety hazards cannot be ignored.

Equity: Science for All

Every school program must ensure equity for every child—regardless of gender, background, learning style, or ability. Equal opportunity to learn often requires *unequal* distribution of time and personnel. Minority students may need role models; at-risk students may need extra attention; and students from language-deprived or non-English speaking backgrounds will need additional time and/or staff in order to participate equally in science classroom experiences.

An important issue relevant to equity is teachers' expectations for their students because children try to achieve what their teachers (and parents) believe they can achieve. Separating and labeling students tends to convey low expectations to students, which in turn often exacerbates low achievement, limits cooperative learning, and eliminates positive student role models for behavior.

Well-intentioned teachers are often totally unaware of the hidden bias in their techniques. For example, many teachers and parents *expect* more males than females to like and excel in science. This expectation is apparent in

classroom observations of questioning, wait-time, assignment of cooperative roles and laboratory tasks, and by textbook examples and visual aids.

Science, for both girls and boys at the elementary level, is most important because these are the years in which the seed of interest in science either falls on rich soil and flourishes or lands on poor soil and withers. It's hard to motivate an older child to like science if sometime between early childhood and adolescence, curiosity, exploration, and motivation were snuffed out.

See Appendix E for more information on equity in the science classroom, especially for students with special needs.

A Community of Learners

The Program Standards describe a new vision for schools: a community of learners that includes students, teachers, parents, administrators, and concerned and interested citizens. Teachers are full partners in

this community. They are the ones who see the systemic barriers to change up close. Because of this unique vantage point, they hold important keys to making changes in school programs and can influence the community.

Bringing About Change

The Standards stress that all science programs should be assessed continually. Like good classroom assessments, program assessments should be woven into the fabric of the program itself, not artificially imposed from without. Teachers should look for indications that students are moving toward the goals that are set by the program.

How does a classroom teacher in an average school district try to move his or her program toward the Standards? It may seem simplistic to say "one step at a time," but many innovations fail because they are too ambitious or try to achieve too much without adequate groundwork and resources. Take a step; assess; then take the next step.

NANCY MARRA

Begin by asking three questions:

#1: *Where do we want to go?*

If the system has not defined consistent goals for *every* course across the curriculum, that's where to begin. Many systems undertaking K–12 program change fail to achieve consistency because they don't start at the beginning—the science the community wants students to know in order for them to be a success as citizens in their community. The beginning of a school science program is to be found *not* in the *courses*, but with the *student*. The question is: what does the community want a graduate of the school district's science program to be able to know and do?

When participants in program review agree on what a graduate should know and be able to do, it is time to chart the contributions of each unit or course to the big picture and write course descriptions. Many schools have found that establishing a common language and format for *every* course in the district is invaluable.

Changing programs is hard work. There are two essential weapons against inertia: one is support from administrators, science supervisors, and peers. The second is that teachers need to know that their work will be appreciated and supported.

#2: *Do support systems exist?*

Many grand proposals fail when support that was promised does not materialize. A district may rewrite a program with heavy emphasis on laboratory skills, but then give the responsibility for buying the materials to school committees with varying commitment to the program, or to principals who have different priorities.

Perhaps even more damaging is the expectation that a quality science program can appear like magic in a system with few resources, inadequate physical accommodations, and with the expectation that teachers will provide their own materials. The keys to effective and long-lasting changes are consistency and realism.

#3: *How are we going to get there?*

This is where the practical experience of teachers is crucial because they can identify changes that need to be made—immediately or soon or in the future. For almost every school, the pathway to a better science program includes professional development. This should never be seen as a one-shot cure for ineffective programming. Staff training must occur before, during, and after implementing a new program.

Taking the Plunge

Trying a new program is a little like skydiving—with the support of peers and the school community as the parachute. Some training is certainly needed before you begin, but once you have some confidence, an experimental jump (in the form of a pilot unit or module) is often just what is needed to build confidence.

To bring about change in school programs, teachers will have to accept positions of leadership. To do that, they will have to believe in themselves.

The pathway to better science programs cannot be walked alone. Together, the professional staff must define their program destination and then chart paths toward goals that parallel and support one another. The Standards provide guiding principles for the journeys teachers must make in their own schools.

Abend, A. C., Bednar, M. J., Froehlinger, V. J. et al. (1979). *Facilities for Special Education Services: A Guide for Planning New and Renovated Schools.* Reston, VA: Council for Exceptional Children.

Allen-Sommerville, Lenola. (1994, March). Middle Level Science in a Multicultural Society. *Science Scope, 17* (6), 16–18.

Atwater, Mary M. (1995, October). The Cross-Curricular Classroom. *Science Scope, 19* (2), 42–45.

Carey, Shelley Johnson (Ed.). (1993). *Science for All Cultures.* Arlington, VA: National Science Teachers Association (NSTA).

Dagher, Zoubeida R. (1995, September). Materials Speak Louder than Words. *Science Scope, 19* (1), 48–50.

Madrazo, Gerry M., Jr., and **Motz, LaMoine L.** (1993). *Sourcebook for Science Supervisors* (4th ed.). Arlington, VA: National Science Teachers Association (NSTA).

Melchert, Sandra A. (1996, February). Bidding Basics for Stretching School Science Dollars. *Science Scope, 19* (5), 34–36.

O'Neil, J. Peter. (1994, March). The Evolving Classroom. *Science Scope, 17* (6), 66–67.

Pederson, Jon E. (1992, May). Take Issue with Science. *Science Scope, 15* (8), 34–37.

Risner, Gregory P., Skeel, Dorothy J., and **Nicholson, Janice I.** (1992, September). A Closer Look at Textbooks. *Science and Children, 30* (1), 42–45, 73.

Roberts, Renee, and **Bazler, Judith A.** (1993, January). Adapting for Disabilities. *The Science Teacher, 60* (1), 22–25.

Safety Supplement. (1989, November/December). *Science Scope, 13* (3), S1–S32.

Showalter, Victor M. (1982). *Conditions for Good Science Teaching.* Arlington, VA: National Science Teachers Association (NSTA).

Technology in the Classroom. (Theme Issue). (March 1996). *Science Scope, 19* (6).

Tennies, Robert H., and **Thielk, Carol K.** (1997, February). The Science Advocate. *Science and Children, 34* (5), 30–31, 40.

Vos, Robert, and **Pell, Sarah W. J.** (1990, December). Limiting Lab Liability. *The Science Teacher, 57* (9), 34–38.

West, Sandra S. (1991, September). Lab Safety. *The Science Teacher, 58* (6), 45–51.

Yager, Robert E. (1992, November/December). Appropriate Science for All. *Science Scope, 16* (3), 57–59.

The full text to most of these resources is available on NSTA's supplementary *Resources for the Road CD-ROM.*

Changing Emphases

The National Science Education Standards envision change throughout the system. The Program Standards encompass the following changes in emphases:

LESS EMPHASIS ON	MORE EMPHASIS ON
Developing science programs at different grade levels independently of one another	Coordinating the development of the K–12 science program across grade levels
Using assessments unrelated to curriculum and teaching	Aligning curriculum, teaching, and assessment
Maintaining current resource allocations for books	Allocating resources necessary for hands-on inquiry teaching aligned with the Standards
Textbook- and lecture-driven curriculum	Curriculum that supports the Standards and includes a variety of components, such as laboratories emphasizing inquiry and field trips
Broad coverage of unconnected factual information	Curriculum that includes natural phenomena and science-related social issues that students encounter in everyday life
Treating science as a subject isolated from other school subjects	Connecting science to other school subjects, such as mathematics and social studies
Science learning opportunities that favor one group of students	Providing challenging opportunities for all students to learn science
Limiting hiring decisions to the administration	Involving successful teachers of science in the hiring process
Maintaining the isolation of teachers	Treating teachers as professionals whose work requires opportunities for continual learning and networking
Supporting competition	Promoting collegiality among teachers as a team to improve the school
Teachers as followers	Teachers as decisionmakers

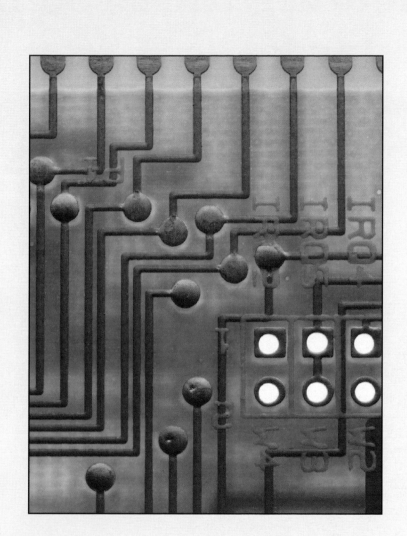

Systems Standards

All parts of the education system must work together and in the process support us in moving toward the vision of the Standards.

Navigating the System Standards

Teachers work magic every day, but by themselves, they cannot move the mountainous education system toward the Science Standards. The *Standards* themselves are adamant on this issue:

"It would be a massive injustice and complete misunderstanding of the Standards if science teachers were left with the full responsibility for implementation. All of the science education community—curriculum developers, superintendents, supervisors, policymakers, assessment specialists, scientists, teacher educators—must act to make the vision of these Standards a reality."

The first step toward any change in education at any level, from the government to the school district to the classroom, is setting the mission. Next, formulating consistent policy at *every* level is critical.

Policies can't be put in place and then sent to schools and teachers to implement without supplying adequate resources and support. Policies must be evaluated constantly for intended and unintended consequences. Even with carefully crafted plans, some unexpected effects, both positive and negative, will occur.

All parts of the education system must work *together* and in the process *support* teachers in moving toward the vision of the Standards. In this policymaking process, *no* stakeholder can be left out. Teachers, administrators, parents, school board members, community members, business and industry representatives, legislators, and representatives of interest groups are *all* important. The Standards themselves provide a common language for all parties to talk about the direction science education should take and reach consensus for action.

Prerequisites for Change

In light of these issues, the seven System Standards set out the following prerequisites for changing the education system to support science education at all levels:

- *Common vision.* Policymakers who influence science education must have a vision that is consistent with the vision of those who coordinate teaching, as-

sessment, professional development, and programs. This vision should also be consistent with the National Science Education Standards.
- *Coordination.* The policies that influence science education should be coordinated across agencies, institutions, and organizations.
- *Continuity.* Policies must be sustained over time so that significant change can be measured against the criteria that have been established.
- *Resources.* Policies must be supported with resources.
- *Equity.* Policies must support equity for all students.
- *Unanticipated effects.* Policies must be examined for possible unintended effects on classroom practice.
- *Individual responsibility.* Responsible individuals will take the opportunity presented by the Standards to move their systems toward reform.

The Power of the Butterfly

There are so many components in the education system, that it is easy to feel powerless. But teachers can take a lesson from modern mathematical chaos theory: When a single butterfly flaps its wings, air currents around the world are affected. In the same way, every contribution, no matter how small, influences the whole.

Elementary teachers and their principals and supervisors should never consider the size of the task an excuse for not beginning reform. There are simple, proven ways to foster change in *every* system and *every* school and classroom.

School reform takes time. The work is best done by teams. A team might be made up of a group of elementary teachers, the principal, district supervisors, parents, students, and community representatives. A good beginning might be the sharing of the importance of science and the vision of the National Science Education Standards.

The Principal Resource

Educating principals about the importance of science (you might begin by sharing this book with them!) can turn principals into advocates for science. Principals working with teachers can set realistic goals, address concerns, and provide time, resources, and training. To spark interest, teachers might invite principals and administrators to take part in science lessons with students or to attend an

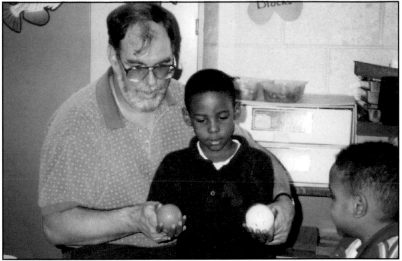

NSTA convention to learn what is possible in elementary science. Principals should be invited to join in preparations for Science Nights and similar events.

Bring Parents to School

Parent involvement is a gold mine for a science program. Parents can be recruited as classroom science instructors bringing their special expertise, or as aides to provide an extra pair of hands, prepare materials, assist during science lessons, help with clean-up, and go on field trips.

Parents are also resources for gaining publicity for the school's science program. They can help locate resources, science materials and supplies, serve as guest speakers if they work in science-related fields, help run a school or district-wide science event, identify local businesses that might be

interested in becoming involved in the science program, monitor experiments, and raise money for equipment. The list is endless.

Parents can carry out investigations, watch videotapes, or listen to audiotapes about science topics with their children. Teachers can develop guidelines for parents to direct discussions about the tapes.

When parents are involved in projects with schools and communities, partnerships are forged that not only maximize resources but also increase support for science. (It is difficult to criticize anything with which you are involved.)

Partner with the Community

Involving community members, including local business people, in the science program also reaps great rewards. Schools may invite business

partners to work together to expand an existing science program. The promise to seek publicity for the business goes a long way in convincing them to join the effort. Businesses may be willing to donate science equipment, mentor students in special projects, or take part in science events. Given the nature of business, the possibilities for cooperation are many.

Working in Teams

In 1992 NSTA coordinated a symposium on change in schools that exemplified the use of teams in fostering change. Through the support of Monsanto Fund, the project developed a model (documented in NSTA's *A Strategy for Change*) for designing systemic reform that incorporates continual monitoring and internal assessment for unanticipated effects.

The NSTA project received applications from 175 school district teams to attend the meeting. Thirty-eight teams were selected and participated in the symposium. Many districts had already begun working on reform, but all were ready for a coordinated self-assessment. The work of the teams emphasized the practical side of systemic reform, and participants were constantly encouraged to look for barriers and unanticipated effects, both positive and negative.

Early on the teams identified what was *needed* to implement change. Then they identified what *hindered* change: time wasted talking and not doing, slow-to-change textbook publishers, little training for teachers in materials management, not enough preparation time in the classroom, and lack of ways to circumvent barriers in school systems. Such insights indicate the value of teacher-based planning.

NSTA interviewed the teams one year after the symposium. Most districts had experienced many of the predicted effects and could cite positive changes. Many reported events they had not anticipated. Anchorage, Alaska, compared its efforts to the ripples formed by a small pebble in a calm lake: The entire community had changed because of the team's work.

The Anchorage analogy of ever-widening ripples in a pond demonstrates the a single change in school science will affect many other areas in ways no one can predict. Planners and teachers must be sensitive to changes, anticipated and unanticipated, and keep their antennae out to sense them. They must be prepared to react and adjust when their intended course changes.

Becoming Active

Ultimately, efforts to change the system must reach beyond individual classrooms and schools. Resisting the old impulse to shut their classroom doors, many teachers are writing and speaking out when proposed changes affect them and their students. The issues that concern them are wide-ranging and include the necessity for providing science teaching materials, federal support for professional development for teachers, and the education of disadvantaged children. Around the nation teachers are running for public office and are using the media to tell the story of school science from their own, unique perspective.

It's Your Turn

Eventually, an opportunity will come to a system near you—an issue, a controversy, or the chance to make a significant change in the way science is taught in *your* school. The challenge may come from a pressure group, from parents, or, ideally, from the message of the National Science Education Standards. What practical steps can elementary teachers take to be part of the process of change?

#1: *Rely on Research*

Share this book and others with those who make decisions. NSTA also offers an awareness kit for administrators on the National Science Education Standards; another kit is available for teachers.

#2: *Bring Friends Along*

Convince colleagues of the importance of activism. As a team, share information and insights.

#3: *Network on the Net*

Access teacher forums on the NSTA Web site, <http://www.nsta.org/>, for quick answers to difficult questions in systemic reform.

#4: *Maintain Professional Memberships*

A major activity of professional organizations is speaking out on issues important to members.

#5: *Call for Support*

If an issue comes before the school board that is so detrimental or so difficult to combat that it threatens good science education, send out a call for help. Your state science supervisor, your NSTA District or Division Director, or your other professional associations can find expert help for you in your area.

It doesn't take a hurricane to move the atmosphere—just the flap of a single butterfly's wings has an effect across the globe. So the involvement of a single teacher can change the system. Given that, imagine the impact of the entire profession speaking with one voice!

ROGER STRYKER

Daisey, Peggy, and **Shroyer, M. Gail.** (1995, November/December). Parents Speak Up. *Science and Children, 33* (3), 24–26.

DeBruin, Jerry, Boellner, Carolyn, Flaskamp, Ruth, and **Sigler, Karen.** (1993, March). Science Investigations Mentorship Program. *Science and Children, 30* (6), 20–22.

Donivan, Marilee. (1993, October). A Dynamic Duo Takes on Science. *Science and Children, 31* (2), 29–32.

Families Involved in Real Science Together. (Theme Issue). (1996, October). *Science and Children, 31* (2).

Gardner, Dara Hallman. (1996, October). Bringing Families and Science Together. *Science and Children, 34* (2), 14–16.

Greenhalgh, Lanai. (1995, September). Youth Teaching Youth. *Science and Children, 33* (1), 35–36, 75.

Halpin, Robert. (1992, April). At Tulip Grove, A Principal for Science. *Science and Children, 29* (7), 34–35.

Ledell, Marjorie, and **Arnsparger, Arleen.** (1993). *How to Deal with Community Criticism of School Change.* Alexandria, VA: Association for Supervision and Curriculum Development (ASCD).

Madrazo, Jr., Gerry M. and **Motz, LaMoine.** *(1993). Sourcebook for Science Supervisors* (4th ed). Arlington, VA: National Science Teachers Association (NSTA).

Mafnas, Irene, Flis, Julie Calvo, and **Dionio, Suzanne.** (1993, September). A Contract for Science. *Science Scope, 17* (1), 45–48.

McCormack, Alan J. (1990, October). The Family Channel. *Science and Children, 28* (2), 24–26.

McLaughlin, Charles W. (1997, February). School to School Partnerships. *Science and Children, 34* (5), 26–29.

Moryan, James. (1994, May). The Corporate Connection. *Science and Children, 31* (8), 18–19, 38.

National Science Teachers Association. (1993). *A Strategy for Change in Elementary School Science: Proceedings of Conference.* Arlington, VA: Author.

North Carolina Museum of Life and Science. (1993). Sharing Science with Children: A Guide for Parents. Durham, NC: Author.

Partnership Possibilities [series of articles in Special Issue: Science in Nontraditional Setting]. (1995, March). *Science Scope, 18* (6), 5–28.

Paulu, Nancy, and **Martin, Margery.** (1992). *Helping Your Child Learn Science.* Washington, DC: U.S. Department of Education, OERI.

Pearlman, Susan, and **Pericak-Spector, Kathleen.** (1993, November/December). A Science Open House. *Science and Children, 31* (3), 12–15.

Pearlman, Susan, and **Pericak-Spector, Kathleen.** (1992, April). Helping Hands from Home. *Science and Children, 29* (7), 12–14.

Public Agenda Foundation. (1993). *Divided Within; Besieged Without: The Politics of Four American School Districts.* New York: Author.

Schwartz, Wendy. (1995, December). Opportunity To Learn Standards: Their Impact on Urban Students. ERIC/CUE Digest No. 110 (ED389816). New York: ERIC Clearinghouse on Urban Education.

Sloan, Gayle. (1993, May). This Principal's Interest Is Science. *Science and Children, 30* (8), 19–20.

Sprague, Jim, and **White, Janet.** (1992, November/December). The Utility Connection. *Science and Children, 30* (3), 16–18.

Sussman, Art (Ed.). (1993). *Science Education Partnerships: Manual for Scientists and K–12 Teachers.* San Francisco: University of California.

Willis, Scott. (1995, June). Responding to Public Opinion: Reforming Schools in a Climate of Skepticism. *Education Update, 37* (5), 1, 2–6.

The full text to most of these resources is available on NSTA's supplementary *Resources for the Road* CD-ROM.

Changing Emphases

District System

LESS EMPHASIS ON	MORE EMPHASIS ON
Technical, short-term, inservice workshops	Ongoing professional development to support teachers
Policies unrelated to Standards-based reform	Policies designed to support changes called for in the Standards
Purchase of textbooks based on traditional topics	Purchase or adoption of curriculum aligned with the Standards and on a conceptual approach to science teaching, including support for hands-on science materials
Standardized tests and assessments unrelated to Standards-based program and practices	Assessments aligned with the Standards
Administration determining what will be involved in improving science education	Teacher leadership in improvement of science education
Authority at upper levels of educational system	Authority for decisions at level of implementation
School board ignorance of science education program	School board support of improvements aligned with the Standards
Local union contracts that ignore changes in curriculum, instruction, and assessment	Local union contracts that support improvements indicated by the Standards

Reprinted with permission from the *National Science Education Standards.* © 1996 National Academy of Sciences. Courtesy of the National Academy Press, Washington, D.C.

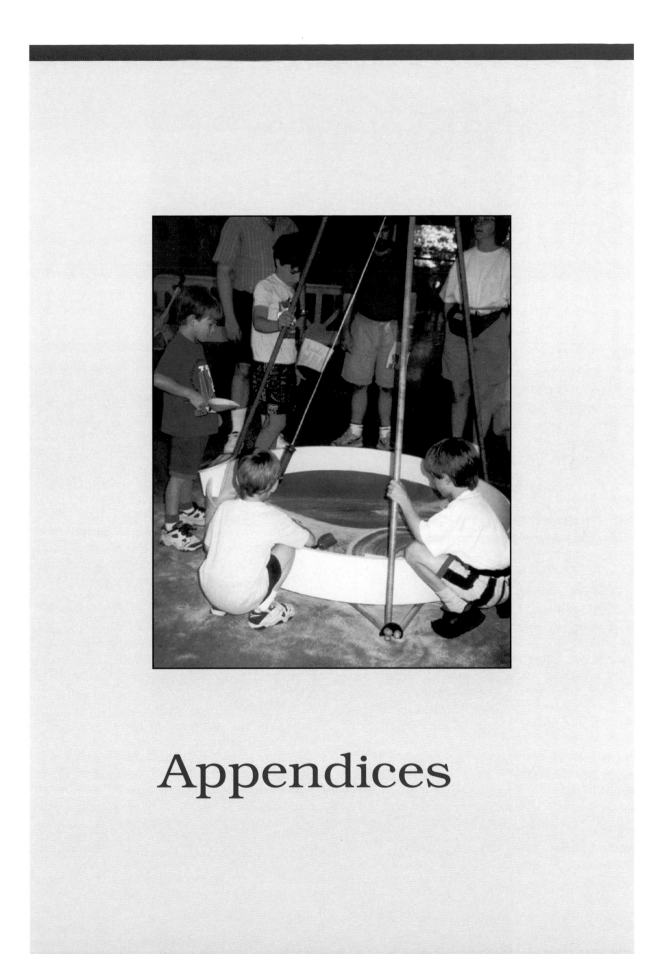

Appendices

Appendix A

National Science Education Standards: Some Relevant History

The publication of the *National Science Education Standards* in December 1995 propelled science education into a new and challenging era. Never before has the practice of science education in the United States been guided by a single set of principles reached by national consensus. The *National Science Education Standards* take their place as a significant contribution to the broad reform movement currently under way in American education.

Precursors to Reform

In April 1983, *A Nation at Risk,* thought to be the most important reform publication of this century, warned that if our education system continued to produce citizens illiterate in science, mathematics, and technology, the nation would lose its influential position in the world, becoming a second-rate power in the 21st century. *A Nation at Risk* sparked a wealth of studies and other efforts that eventually coalesced into a significant broad-based reform movement in education.

Among the first studies were efforts to compare the literacy levels of U.S. students with those of students in other countries. Although many of the studies were poorly designed, making their findings invalid, the better studies consistently found a need to improve the teaching of science and mathematics in this country.

Launching Reform

Among the various efforts to reform science education was Project 2061, initiated in 1986 by the American Association for the Advancement of Science. This project takes a long-term view of science education reform. The project's goal is to develop a high level of science literacy among all American citizens. Its first publication, *Science for All Americans* (1989), outlined the understanding and habit of mind necessary for a scientifically literate citizen. In 1993, Project 2061 released *Benchmarks for Science Literacy,* which established minimum goals for what students should know and be able to do at various grade levels in a number of content areas.

In 1989, NSTA launched its Scope, Sequence, and Coordination of Secondary School Science project (SS&C). The NSTA curriculum reform project sought to revamp the layercake approach to the study of science (a different science every year). Instead, a curriculum based on the principles of SS&C would give students carefully sequenced (from concrete to abstract, paralleling student development), well-coordinated instruction in *all* the sciences *every* year. The SS&C approach is currently being field-tested at the high school level. Previous efforts focused on the middle grades. Publications of this project include *The Content Core, Relevant Research*, and *A High School Framework for Science Education.*

Goals and Standards

While these efforts were going on, two other events were propelling the nation toward setting Standards for school subjects. In 1989, after three years of work, the National Council of Teachers of Mathematics released its *Curriculum and Evaluation Standards for School Mathematics*. Its goal was to revolutionize the teaching of mathematics as a subject for *all* students, not just those who were college-bound.

About the same time President Bush decided to convene an education summit of the nation's governors. From this summit came an agreement that national goals for education should be set. The National Governors' Association and the President developed the National Education Goals, which were released in the State of the Union address in early 1990. According to Goal 4, "By the year 2000, U.S. students will be first in the world in science and mathematics achievement."

The National Education Goals Panel was established to monitor progress toward each of the goals. President Bush launched the America 2000 effort to get communities involved in working toward the goals. (Later, President Clinton would continue these goal-directed efforts, renaming the program Goals 2000.)

The need to set *voluntary* national Standards for what all students should know and be able to do at various grade levels in the subjects addressed by the goals soon became apparent. These included science, mathematics, English, history, civics and government, geography, economics, foreign languages, and the arts. Standards-setting projects, often with funding from agencies of the federal government, were quickly launched in these subjects, including science.

Toward Consensus in Science

In spring 1991, the president of NSTA, with the unanimous support of the NSTA board of directors, wrote to Frank Press, president of the National Academy of Sciences and chair of the National Research Council (NRC), asking NRC to coordinate the development of national Standards in science education. The presidents of other leading science and science education associations, the U.S. Secretary of Education, the assistant director for education and human resources at the National Science Foundation (NSF), and the co-chairs of the National Education Goals Panel also encouraged NRC to play a leading role. NRC agreed; and shortly thereafter, major funding for the project was provided by the Department of Education and NSF. Other funders included NASA, the U.S. Department of Energy, the U.S. Department of Agriculture, and the National Institutes of Health.

NRC began its work by convening the National Committee on Science Education Standards and Assessment and the Chair's Advisory Committee, consisting of representatives from the major science and science education associations. This group helped to identify and to recruit staff and volunteers for all the Standards-writing working groups.

The three working groups—content Standards, teaching Standards, and assessment Standards—set to work in summer 1992 and over the next 18 months, solicited input from large numbers of teachers, scientists, science educators, and many others interested in science education.

In spring 1993, a pre-draft of the Science Education Standards was released to selected focus groups for critique and review. Comments were collated and analyzed; and in December 1994, more than 40,000 copies of the draft *National Science Education Standards* were distributed nationwide to some 18,000 individuals and 250 groups. Again, comments were collated and analyzed, and the *National Science Education Standards* was published in December 1995.

The Science Standards provide a vision, *not* a curriculum, for science education. They are descriptive, *not* prescriptive. One of the strongest principles underlying the Standards is that science is for *all* students in all grades.

Release of the *National Science Education Standards* is a pivotal event for teachers of science and those they work with—from students and parents to administrators and legislators. The Standards present clearly what *can* be done but leave the nuts and bolts of implementation to individual choice and responsibility. The *Standards* clearly state that all the Standards should be taken together as a package—implementation should not be done cafeteria-style. And finally, the responsibility for putting the vision of the Standards into action belongs to *everyone* in science education: teachers, curriculum developers, superintendents, administrators, supervisors, policymakers, assessment specialists, scientists, teacher educators, parents, businesses, and local communities.

RESOURCES FOR THE ROAD

American Association for the Advancement of Science (AAAS), Project 2061. (1989). *Science for All Americans.* New York: Oxford University Press.

American Association for the Advancement of Science (AAAS), Project 2061. (1993). *Benchmarks for Science Literacy.* New York: Oxford University Press.

Aldridge, Bill G. (Ed.) (1996). *Scope, Sequence, and Coordination: A High School Framework for Science Education.* Arlington, VA: National Science Teachers Association (NSTA).

National Commission on Excellence in Education. (1983). *A Nation at Risk: The Imperative for Educational Reform.* Washington, DC: Author.

National Council of Teachers of Mathematics (NCTM). (1989). *Curriculum and Evaluation Standards for School Mathematics.* Reston, VA: Author.

National Council of Teachers of Mathematics (NCTM). (1989). *Professional Standards for Teaching Mathematics.* Reston, VA: Author.

National Science Teachers Association (NSTA). (1998). *NSTA's Pathways to the Science Standards, High School Edition.* Arlington, VA: Author.

National Science Teachers Association (NSTA). (1998). *Resources for the Road CD-ROM* Arlington, VA: Author.

National Science Teachers Association (NSTA). (2000). *NSTA's Pathways to the Science Standards, Middle School Edition, 2nd Edition.* Arlington, VA: Author.

Appendix B
National Science Education Standards

Principles

- Science is for all students.
- Learning science is an active process.
- School science reflects the intellectual and cultural traditions that characterize the practice of contemporary science.
- Improving science education is part of systemic education reform.

Science Teaching Standards

TEACHING STANDARD A: Teachers of science plan an inquiry-based science program for their students. In doing this, teachers
- Develop a framework of year-long and short-term goals for students
- Select science content and adapt and design curricula to meet the interests, knowledge, understanding, abilities, and experiences of students
- Select teaching and assessment strategies that support the development of student understanding and nurture a community of science learners
- Work together as colleagues within and across disciplines and grade levels

TEACHING STANDARD B: Teachers of science guide and facilitate learning. In doing this, teachers
- Focus and support inquiries while interacting with students
- Orchestrate discourse among students about scientific ideas
- Challenge students to accept and share responsibility for their own learning
- Recognize and respond to student diversity and encourage all students to participate fully in science learning

- Encourage and model the skills of scientific inquiry, as well as the curiosity, openness to new ideas and data, and skepticism that characterize science

TEACHING STANDARD C: Teachers of science engage in ongoing assessment of their teaching and of student learning. In doing this, teachers
- Use multiple methods and systematically gather data about student understanding and ability
- Analyze assessment data to guide teaching
- Guide students in self-assessment
- Use student data, observations of teaching, and interactions with colleagues to reflect on and improve teaching practice
- Use student data, observations of teaching, and interactions with colleagues to report student achievement and opportunities to learn to students, teachers, parents, policymakers, and the general public

TEACHING STANDARD D: Teachers of science design and manage learning environments that provide students with the time, space, and resources needed for learning science. In doing this, teachers
- Structure the time available so that students are able to engage in extended investigations
- Create a setting for student work that is flexible and supportive of science inquiry
- Ensure a safe working environment
- Make the available science tools, materials, media, and technological resources accessible to students
- Identify and use resources outside the school
- Engage students in designing the learning environment

TEACHING STANDARD E: Teachers of science develop communities of science learners that reflect the intellectual rigor of scientific inquiry and the attitudes and social values conducive to science learning. In doing this, teachers

- Display and demand respect for the diverse ideas, skills, and experiences of all students
- Enable students to have a significant voice in decisions about the content and context of their work and require students to take responsibility for the learning of all members of the community
- Nurture collaboration among students
- Structure and facilitate ongoing formal and informal discussion based on a shared understanding of rules of scientific discourse
- Model and emphasize the skills, attitudes, and values of scientific inquiry

TEACHING STANDARD F: Teachers of science actively participate in the ongoing planning and development of the school science program. In doing this, teachers

- Plan and develop the school science program
- Participate in decisions concerning the allocation of time and other resources to the science program
- Participate fully in planning and implementing professional growth and development strategies for themselves and their colleagues

Standards for Professional Development for Teachers of Science

PROFESSIONAL DEVELOPMENT STANDARD A: Professional development for teachers of science requires learning essential science content through the perspectives and methods of inquiry. Science learning experiences for teachers must

- Involve teachers in actively investigating phenomena that can be studied scientifically, interpreting results, and making sense of findings consistent with currently accepted scientific understanding
- Address issues, events, problems, or topics significant in science and of interest to participants
- Introduce teachers to scientific literature, media, and technological resources that

expand their science knowledge and their ability to access further knowledge

- Build on the teacher's current science understanding, ability, and attitudes
- Incorporate ongoing reflection on the process and outcomes of understanding science through inquiry
- Encourage and support teachers in efforts to collaborate

PROFESSIONAL DEVELOPMENT STANDARD B: Professional development for teachers of science requires integrating knowledge of science, learning, pedagogy, and students; it also requires applying that knowledge to science teaching. Learning experiences for teachers of science must

- Connect and integrate all pertinent aspects of science and science education
- Occur in a variety of places where effective science teaching can be illustrated and modeled, permitting teachers to struggle with real situations and expand their knowledge and skills in appropriate contexts
- Address teachers' needs as learners and build on their current knowledge of science content, teaching, and learning
- Use inquiry, reflection, interpretation of research, modeling, and guided practice to build understanding and skill in science teaching

PROFESSIONAL DEVELOPMENT STANDARD C: Professional development for teachers of science requires building understanding and ability for lifelong learning. Professional development activities must

- Provide regular, frequent opportunities for individual and collegial examination and reflection on classroom and institutional practice
- Provide opportunities for teachers to receive feedback about their teaching and to understand, analyze, and apply that feedback to improve their practice
- Provide opportunities for teachers to learn and use various tools and techniques for self-reflection and collegial reflection, such as peer coaching, portfolios, and journals
- Support the sharing of teacher expertise by preparing and using mentors, teacher advisors, coaches, lead teachers, and resource

teachers to provide professional development opportunities

- Provide opportunities to know and have access to existing research and experiential knowledge
- Provide opportunities to learn and use the skills of research to generate new knowledge about science and the teaching and learning of science

PROFESSIONAL DEVELOPMENT STANDARD D: Professional development programs for teachers of science must be coherent and integrated. Quality preservice and inservice programs are characterized by

- Clear, shared goals based on a vision of science learning, teaching, and teacher development congruent with the *National Science Education Standards*
- Integration and coordination of the program components so that understanding and ability can be built over time, reinforced continuously, and practiced in a variety of situations
- Options that recognize the developmental nature of teacher professional growth and individual and group interests, as well as the needs of teachers who have varying degrees of experience, professional expertise, and proficiency
- Collaboration among the people involved in programs, including teachers, teacher educators, teacher unions, scientists, administrators, policymakers, members of professional and scientific organizations, parents, and businesspeople, with clear respect for the perspectives and expertise of each
- Recognition of the history, culture, and organization of the school environment
- Continuous program assessment that captures the perspectives of all those involved, uses a variety of strategies, focuses on the process and effects of the program, and feeds directly into program improvement and evaluation

Standards for Assessment in Science Education

ASSESSMENT STANDARD A: Assessments must be consistent with the decisions they are designed to inform.

- Assessments are deliberately designed.
- Assessments have explicitly stated purposes.
- The relationship between the decisions and the data is clear.
- Assessment procedures are internally consistent.

ASSESSMENT STANDARD B: Achievement and opportunity to learn science must be assessed.

- Achievement data collected focus on the science content that is most important for students to learn.
- Opportunity-to-learn data collected focus on the most powerful indicators.
- Equal attention must be given to the assessment of opportunity to learn and to the assessment of student achievement.

ASSESSMENT STANDARD C: The technical quality of the data collected is well matched to the decisions and actions taken on the basis of their interpretation.

- The feature that is claimed to be measured is actually measured.
- Assessment tasks are authentic.
- An individual student's performance is similar on two or more tasks that claim to measure the same aspect of student achievement.
- Students have adequate opportunity to demonstrate their achievements.
- Assessment tasks and methods of presenting them provide data that are sufficiently stable to lead to the same decisions if used at different times.

ASSESSMENT STANDARD D: Assessment practices must be fair.

- Assessment tasks must be reviewed for the use of stereotypes, for assumptions that reflect the perspectives or experiences of a particular group, for language that might be offensive to a particular group, and for other features that might distract students from the intended task.
- Large-scale assessments must use statistical techniques to identify potential bias among subgroups.
- Assessment tasks must be appropriately

modified to accommodate the needs of students with physical disabilities, learning disabilities, or limited English proficiency.
- Assessment tasks must be set in a variety of contexts, be engaging to students with different interests and experiences, and must not assume the perspective or experience of a particular gender, racial, or ethnic group.

ASSESSMENT STANDARD E: The inferences made from assessments about student achievement and opportunity to learn must be sound.
- When making inferences from assessment data about student achievement and opportunity to learn science, explicit reference needs to be made to the assumptions on which the inferences are based.

Science Content Standards

Content Standard: K–12

Unifying Concepts and Processes

STANDARD: As a result of activities in grades K–12, all students should develop understanding and abilities aligned with the following concepts and processes:
- Systems, order, and organization
- Evidence, models, and explanation
- Constancy, change, and measurement
- Evolution and equilibrium
- Form and function

Content Standards: K–4

Science as Inquiry

CONTENT STANDARD A: As a result of activities in grades K–4, all students should develop
- Abilities necessary to do scientific inquiry
- Understanding about scientific inquiry

Physical Science

CONTENT STANDARD B: As a result of the activities in grades K–4, all students should develop an understanding of
- Properties of objects and materials
- Position and motion of objects
- Light, heat, electricity, and magnetism

Life Science

CONTENT STANDARD C: As a result of activities in grades K–4, all students should develop understanding of
- The characteristics of organisms
- Life cycles of organisms
- Organisms and environments

Earth and Space Science

CONTENT STANDARD D: As a result of their activities in grades K–4, all students should develop an understanding of
- Properties of earth materials
- Objects in the sky
- Changes in earth and sky

Science and Technology

CONTENT STANDARD E: As a result of activities in grades K–4, all students should develop
- Abilities of technological design
- Understanding about science and technology
- Abilities to distinguish between natural objects and objects made by humans

Science in Personal and Social Perspectives

CONTENT STANDARD F: As a result of activities in grades K–4, all students should develop understanding of
- Personal health
- Characteristics and changes in populations
- Types of resources
- Changes in environments
- Science and technology in local challenges

History and Nature of Science

CONTENT STANDARD G: As a result of activities in grades K–4, all students should develop understanding of
- Science as a human endeavor

Content Standards: 5–8

Science as Inquiry

CONTENT STANDARD A: As a result of activities in grades 5–8, all students should develop
- Abilities necessary to do scientific inquiry
- Understandings about scientific inquiry

Physical Science

CONTENT STANDARD B: As a result of their activities in grades 5–8, all students should develop an understanding of
- Properties and changes of properties in matter
- Motions and forces
- Transfer of energy

Life Science

CONTENT STANDARD C: As a result of their activities in grades 5–8, all students should develop understanding of
- Structure and function in living systems
- Reproduction and heredity
- Regulation and behavior
- Populations and ecosystems
- Diversity and adaptations of organisms

Earth and Space Science

CONTENT STANDARD D: As a result of their activities in grades 5–8, all students should develop an understanding of
- Structure of the earth system
- Earth's history
- Earth in the solar system

Science and Technology

CONTENT STANDARD E: As a result of activities in grades 5–8, all students should develop
- Abilities of technological design
- Understandings about science and technology

Science in Personal and Social Perspectives

CONTENT STANDARD F: As a result of activities in grades 5–8, all students should develop understanding of
- Personal health
- Populations, resources, and environments
- Natural hazards
- Risks and benefits
- Science and technology in society

History and Nature of Science

CONTENT STANDARD G: As a result of activities in grades 5–8, all students should develop understanding of
- Science as a human endeavor

- Nature of science
- History of science

Content Standards: 9–12

Science as Inquiry

CONTENT STANDARD A: As a result of activities in grades 9–12, all students should develop
- Abilities necessary to do scientific inquiry
- Understandings about scientific inquiry

Physical Science

CONTENT STANDARD B: As a result of their activities in grades 9–12, all students should develop an understanding of
- Structure of atoms
- Structure and properties of matter
- Chemical reactions
- Motions and forces
- Conservation of energy and increase in disorder
- Interactions of energy and matter

Life Science

CONTENT STANDARD C: As a result of their activities in grades 9–12, all students should develop understanding of
- The cell
- Molecular basis of heredity
- Biological evolution
- Interdependence of organisms
- Matter, energy, and organization in living systems
- Behavior of organisms

Earth and Space Science

CONTENT STANDARD D: As a result of their activities in grades 9–12, all students should develop an understanding of
- Energy in the earth system
- Geochemical cycles
- Origin and evolution of the earth system
- Origin and evolution of the universe

Science and Technology

CONTENT STANDARD E: As a result of activities in grades 9–12, all students should develop
- Abilities of technological design

- Understandings about science and technology

Science in Personal and Social Perspectives

CONTENT STANDARD F: As a result of activities in grades 9–12, all students should develop understanding of
- Personal and community health
- Population growth
- Natural resources
- Environmental quality
- Natural and human-induced hazards
- Science and technology in local, national, and global challenges

History and Nature of Science

CONTENT STANDARD G: As a result of activities in grades 9–12, all students should develop understanding of
- Science as a human endeavor
- Nature of scientific knowledge
- Historical perspectives

Science Education Program Standards

PROGRAM STANDARD A: All elements of the K–12 science program must be consistent with the other *National Science Education Standards* and with one another and developed within and across grade levels to meet a clearly stated set of goals.
- In an effective science program, a set of clear goals and expectations for students must be used to guide the design, implementation, and assessment of all elements of the science program.
- Curriculum frameworks should be used to guide the selection and development of units and courses of study.
- Teaching practices need to be consistent with the goals and curriculum frameworks.
- Assessment policies and practices should be aligned with the goals, student expectations, and curriculum frameworks.
- Support systems and formal and informal expectations of teachers must be aligned with the goals, student expectations, and curriculum frameworks.
- Responsibility needs to be clearly defined for determining, supporting, maintaining, and upgrading all elements of the science program.

PROGRAM STANDARD B: The program of study in science for all students should be developmentally appropriate, interesting, and relevant to students' lives; emphasize student understanding through inquiry; and be connected with other school subjects.
- The program of study should include all of the content standards.
- Science content must be embedded in a variety of curriculum patterns that are developmentally appropriate, interesting, and relevant to students' lives.
- The program of study must emphasize student understanding through inquiry.
- The program of study in science should connect to other school subjects.

PROGRAM STANDARD C: The science program should be coordinated with the mathematics program to enhance student use and understanding of mathematics in the study of science and to improve student understanding of mathematics.

PROGRAM STANDARD D: The K–12 science program must give students access to appropriate and sufficient resources, including quality teachers, time, materials and equipment, adequate and safe space, and the community.
- The most important resource is professional teachers.
- Time is a major resource in a science program.
- Conducting scientific inquiry requires that students have easy, equitable, and frequent opportunities to use a wide range of equipment, materials, supplies, and other resources for experimentation and direct investigation of phenomena.
- Collaborative inquiry requires adequate and safe space.
- Good science programs require access to the world beyond the classroom.

PROGRAM STANDARD E: All students in the K–12 science program must have equitable access to opportunities to achieve the *National Science Education Standards*.

PROGRAM STANDARD F: Schools must work as communities that encourage, support, and sustain teachers as they implement an effective science program.

- Schools must explicitly support reform efforts in an atmosphere of openness and trust that encourages collegiality.
- Regular time needs to be provided and teachers encouraged to discuss, reflect, and conduct research around science education reform.
- Teachers must be supported in creating and being members of networks of reform.
- An effective leadership structure that includes teachers must be in place.

Science Education System Standards

SYSTEM STANDARD A: Policies that influence the practice of science education must be congruent with the program, teaching, professional development, assessment, and content standards while allowing for adaptation to local circumstances.

SYSTEM STANDARD B: Policies that influence science education should be coordinated within and across agencies, institutions, and organizations.

SYSTEM STANDARD C: Policies need to be sustained over sufficient time to provide the continuity necessary to bring about the changes required by the *Standards*.

SYSTEM STANDARD D: Policies must be supported with resources.

SYSTEM STANDARD E: Science education policies must be equitable.

SYSTEM STANDARD F: All policy instruments must be reviewed for possible unintended effects on the classroom practice of science education.

SYSTEM STANDARD G: Responsible individuals must take the opportunity afforded by the standards-based reform movement to achieve the new vision of science education portrayed in the *Standards*.

EMILY W. KING

Appendix C

Designing Elementary School Science Facilities

Program Standard D: *The K–12 science program must give students access to appropriate and sufficient resources, including quality teachers, time, materials and equipment, adequate and safe space, and the community.*

The *NSTA Guide to School Science Facilities* (Biehle, Motz, and West, 1999) will help you design and build your science classroom and laboratory. What follows is a summary of that book.

Proper facilities are an essential resource for effective science investigations and instruction and the first line of defense in providing a safe science education environment. No curriculum, system of discipline, or instructional strategy can fully overcome the limitations resulting from inadequate facilities.

Elementary students need concrete experiences with scientific phenomena to understand basic science concepts and principles. The *National Science Education Standards* calls time, space, and materials "critical components" for promoting sustained inquiry.

Inductive inquiry/discovery and deductive laboratory and field activities require similar facilities and equipment. At the elementary level, science is most often taught in self-contained, multiple-use classrooms, but in some schools specialized science rooms or resource centers are available. Whatever the form of the science room, safety, flexibility, and other needs and requirements must be taken into account.

The following sections offer several criteria for creating a science learning environment that encourages maximum student involvement and achievement and assists teachers in their work toward achieving the Standards.

Class Time

It is important to allot sufficient time for hands-on exploratory activities and an accompanying discussion and explanation of the science concepts involved. Plan for a minimum of 150 minutes per week of science instruction in grades 1–3 and 225 minutes in grades 4–6, including science work that is part of an integrated curriculum, with at least 60 percent of science instructional time devoted to hands-on experiences in the field or laboratory.

Planning for Facilities Design

Planning involves discussion, investigation, and decisionmaking to determine the physical environment the science program requires. A participatory process that encourages input from diverse groups is most likely to result in a facility design that is specific to the district, curriculum, and program and that will have community support.

Before decisions on design and location of science facilities are made, it is important to determine exactly how science will be taught.

Participants

The planning committee for construction, addition, or renovation of elementary-level facilities typically includes the principal, elementary teachers, representative parents and students, the science supervisor, and the superintendent or assistant superintendent. In addition, the following groups may be represented on the committee or be involved in various aspects of planning:
• science specialists

- science facilities specialists
- school administrators
- a university-based consultant
- school support services personnel
- architects
- furniture consultants
- community members
- business leaders

If the project requires specific votes or approvals by the local government, consult with appropriate officials and political leaders from the start. Include custodians and facilities maintenance staff in discussions; they have a stake in the final product and can contribute practical suggestions to ensure that the facilities can be kept in good working order long after the project is completed.

Bring special education staff members and parents of special education students into the process for their expertise in identifying accessibility issues. The district or municipality should have a specialist knowledgeable about the Americans With Disabilities Act (ADA) requirements. Consult with this person because he or she can offer suggestions and advise architects of methods of compliance.

Preparation

Prior to beginning their work with designers, architects, and engineers, teachers and supervisors who will serve on the planning committee should try to acquire a background in understanding
- how the design and construction process works
- what factors affect construction costs
- how to read plans and specifications

A subcommittee could be formed to gather input from the community and raise community awareness. The subcommittee could develop a questionnaire and administer it to a group of students, educators, parents, and community representatives. The questionnaire should address areas of exemplary and safe science instruction identified as presented by the National Science Education Standards, the elementary science curriculum, and state and local regulations.

Planning

The planning committee prepares a statement of needs and educational specifications that will provide the foundation for design and development. Checklists are useful at this stage to help ensure that various building, design, funding eligibility, space, equipment, and safety requirements are met.

Determine enrollment projections for short-term, mid-term, and long-term needs. If a population surge is anticipated, determine whether the bulge can be accommodated on a temporary (5- to 10-year) basis; if so, plan facilities that allow for low-cost modification for other uses in future years. For new construction or major renovations, a 20-year projection of needs should be developed.

Planning and design considerations include the following:
- the nature of the science taught and the overall educational program
- desired characteristics of the science facilities
- number of science facilities needed
- clustering of facilities
- safety requirements
- furnishings and equipment
- proposed computer usage and other technology needs
- outdoor education areas
- adaptations for students with disabilities
- government regulations
- maintenance requirements
- budget
- time line

Budget Priorities

The maxim "pay now or pay more later" applies here. A foundation for academic excellence begins with excellent facilities. They are not a luxury, but a requirement for maximum student achievement.

Space and safety are primary considerations in the planning budget. Lack of adequate space is much more costly to address later than the purchase of additional equipment, furniture, or new technology; also, overcrowding risks accidents and litigation. Any safety hazards resulting from poorly designed facilities will likely cause problems for the life of the building. In addition, good planning dictates that wiring and other accommodations for electronic resources take into account both current and future needs.

Annual science budgets need to support operating costs, equipment maintenance and acquisition, and supplies.

Space Considerations

Space is an important factor in promoting inquiry, collaborative learning, and safety. Considering current technology needs and teaching practices, a good science room will require

- a minimum of 3.6 m² (40 ft.²) per student, which is equivalent to 89.2 m² (960 ft.²), to safely accommodate a class of 24. (The 1990 NSTA Position Statement on Laboratory Science recommends a maximum class size of 24 students in elementary school.)
- additional space to accommodate students with disabilities
- 1.4 m² (15 ft.²) for each computer station with monitor, keyboard, CPU, printer, and CD-ROM
- 1.1 m² (12 ft.²) for a multimedia projector or data projector with a hard drive

In addition, 0.9 m² (10 ft.²) per student is needed for preparation space for the teacher and separate storage space (22 m², or 240 ft.², for a class of 24).

General Room Design

The design of an effective science room accommodates work in all science disciplines, with flexibility in furniture arrangement, abundant storage, sufficient working space for the safe conduct of activities, and holding space for ongoing projects. A rectangular room that is closer to being square works better than a long, narrow one. The room must have at least two exits and unobstructed doorways wide enough to accommodate students with

physical disabilities. A ceiling height of 3 m (10 ft.) is desirable. Adequate ventilation (a minimum of four air changes per hour) is also important.

In addition to furnishings, equipment, wiring, and ventilation (discussed below), additional factors to consider are space for teacher planning, a view of the outdoors, daylight exposure (preferably southern) for plant growth, and the inclusion of a projecting plant window. Heating and cooling systems are necessary for year-round use of facilities.

Furnishings for the Multiple-Use Classroom

If science is to be taught in a self-contained, multiple-use classroom, the following are needed:

- a large sink with hot and cold water, at an appropriate height for students, located on the classroom perimeter, with adjacent counter space
- additional sinks or "wet areas"
- at least one rolling cart with tote-tray for storage and distribution of science supplies and materials
- counter surfaces and/or rolling carts with racks for storage of materials used in ongoing experiments
- two- or four-student tables
- display areas with manipulative materials accessible to students
- chalkboard or marker board and tackable wall surfaces for the display of charts and posters
- base and wall cabinets and shelves for storage
- lockable cabinets or storage closet (in the classroom or elsewhere)
- electrical outlets with ground-fault-interrupter protection at frequent intervals around the perimeter of the classroom
- provisions for electronic communications, as desired
- space for an eye wash

Many of these resources can serve multiple curricular goals. For details and other suggestions, see the following recommendations for the specialized science classroom.

Furnishings for the Specialized Science Classroom

A room dedicated to science instruction can offer additional resources and customized work and storage space. The following describes a science room with movable tables and perimeter counters, sinks, and utilities for maximum flexibility in the use of space. Fixed lab stations or service islands require more space, and sight lines may not be as good.

Sinks and Work Space

A large, deep sink with a rubber mat, hot and cold water, and 1.8 m (6 linear ft.) of adjacent counter space is needed for preparation for safety reasons and is useful for demonstrations. Students' science investigations and cleanup require four or five sinks with water outlets along perimeter countertops or peninsulas.

Provide movable, flat-topped desks or two-student tables. Four-student tables are also satisfactory. Countertops 69 to 74 cm (27 to 29 in.) above the floor are convenient for most elementary students, and tables 51 to 58 cm (20 to 23 in.) high for students up to fifth grade, 61 cm (24 in.) high for sixth graders, are appropriate. Chairs of a variety of seat heights can accommodate students of various heights. Ideally, all countertops and other top surfaces in classrooms, preparation rooms, and storerooms will have durable finishes resistant to water and mild chemicals.

Storage and Wall Space

Provide base cabinets with student-level counters along at least two walls for additional work and preparation space. All shelves and wall cabinets should be placed above base cabinets for safety reasons. Avoid particleboard assembly for casework unless a special sealant is used because it is prone to problems with water penetration.

Chalkboards or marker boards and tackable wall surfaces for maps and posters are also needed. Allot space for an eye wash and floor space for equipment. For specialized storage, consider a storage closet (preferably at least 1.8 by 2.4 m, or 6 by 8 ft.), shelves, cabinets of various sizes and shapes, and at least 5.5 m (18 linear ft.) of bookshelves. Make sure enough lockable cabinets are available for teacher use and for storing student projects. Shelving at least 25 cm (10 in.) deep for books and 38 to 46 cm (15 to 18 in.) deep for equipment should be provided, mounted on stands that allow adjustment to different heights. Ceiling hooks are useful for hanging demonstration and experimental apparatus.

If there is a pull-down audiovisual screen, it may be mounted at an angle in a front corner of the room, so that its use does not block the view of the chalkboard.

Lighting and Wiring

Six covered, duplex electrical outlets with ground-fault-interrupter protection are needed at countertop height for the work spaces near the sinks, and additional outlets with ground-fault protection should be spaced frequently along the other walls for convenient use. Provide wall outlets or recessed electrical floor boxes for computers and other equipment, as needed. Computers require separate circuits with surge protection and grounding. Also provide data connections to the school's computer network (or conduit and outlets for future connection) and wiring for voice, data, and video communications, as desired. A telephone or other provision for emergency help should be available in the science room or nearby.

The emergency shut-off controls for water and electrical service should be near the teacher's station, not far from the door, and not easily accessible to students. Master controls may include electric solenoid with key reactivation.

Lighting of a minimum of 50 foot-candles per square foot of floor surface (and 75 to 100 foot-candles at the work surface) is needed, as well as an emergency light (if adequate natural light is not available) in case of an electricity failure. Room-darkening shades with edge tracks are desirable for various science activities. Provide a dimmer switch to control lights in the front half of the room for use with audiovisual equipment, or install three-tube fluorescent lighting, separately switched, so that one, two, or three tubes can be on at a time. Consider fluorescent lighting with parabolic lenses to reduce the glare on computer screens.

Equipment and Supplies

A source of heat, such as gas, hot plate, or microwave oven, should be available for the teacher's use. Computers and appropriate software, a CD-ROM player, and an overhead projector are needed, as well as science materials and equipment such as magnets, thermometers, two-pan balances, measuring tools, models, plastic beakers, and containers. Provide hand lenses for every student. A television monitor, VCR, and videodisc player are also recommended. A good CD-ROM science program on one or two computers is useful for small-group activities. For upper elementary students, laptop computers with probeware, word-processing, and database software are desirable for use in field and outdoor studies as well as in the laboratory.

The following laboratory and field equipment is strongly recommended:
- aquariums, terraria, vivaria
- animal cages or study center
- binocular or stereomicroscopes
- supply carts
- maps and globes
- astronomy equipment
- weather instruments
- stream table
- microslide viewers
- tripod magnifiers
- egg incubator
- germination/growth chamber

The following are recommended:
- a clock with a sweep second hand

- photography equipment
- videomicroscope
- refrigerator
- dishwasher

Microbiological incubators are not recommended at the elementary level because they present an unnecessary hazard.

Make arrangements to ensure adequate year-round care of animals, including backup heating and cooling systems for vacation periods.

Preparation and Storage Rooms

A separate preparation room for the teacher is desirable. Ideally, it should be adjacent to the science room and storage areas. Consider providing a view window between the preparation and science rooms to facilitate supervision of students. Adequate ventilation and safety equipment are required. Provide a large, deep sink and a variety of shelves and cabinets. If a microwave oven is needed for demonstrations, it is best located in the preparation room. Chemicals should not be stored in the preparation room but should be kept in a separate, secure, ventilated storage closet.

Storage rooms supplement the storage areas in science rooms and provide needed security and specialized storage for large, expensive, or sensitive equipment.

If needed, a dedicated, locked chemical storage area that is well ventilated (12 air changes per hour forced-air ventilation) should be provided. Separation of incompatible materials is important, as well as special precautions for flammable materials. Design shelves to inhibit spread of spills, and use wood or other corrosion-resistant materials for the shelves and any attachments. It is desirable to limit shelf depth to 12 in. (30 cm) to prevent the storage of multiple bottles behind one another. Chemicals should not be stored in the same room with equipment or master shut-off controls because the chemicals could corrode metal parts.

Safety Considerations

For safety reasons, adequate circulation space and strict observation of the limit on class size are important. For students' protection, enclose utility lines that are above or below any service islands.

The science room should have splash-proof personal safety goggles for all students and adults (as needed), physician-approved first-aid kit, centrally located dual eyewash that will provide a tempered flow of aerated water for at least 15 minutes, ABC fire extinguisher at each exit, and smoke/heat detectors. Providing one sink with soap dispenser for every four or five students also improves safety in the science room. It is a good idea to install a lip edge on any open shelves used for storing bottles or chemicals.

The science room requires at least two locking entrances and adequate ventilation. For maximum safety, provide two locking entrances for all storage and preparation areas as well.

Be sure to provide supervision of custodians who clean chemical storage areas unless they have had specific training.

Earthquake Precautions

Recommendations and requirements for earthquake and hurricane precautions for school facilities can be obtained from the state disaster department.

Because books and equipment will fall off open shelves during earthquakes, cabinets with hinged doors and positive latches are recommended in areas subject to seismic activity. These cabinets should be bolted to walls and partitions. Deep tracks will help prevent sliding cabinet doors from being jolted out of their tracks by the upward motion of an earthquake. Lips or rods can help keep items from sliding off shelves; ideally, shelving for chemical storage will have individual recesses for each container.

It is advisable to clamp or bolt equipment to counters wherever possible. If computers are mounted on carts, the carts may be kept in cabinets when not in use. Major building codes specify requirements for walls, ceilings, and equipment.

Adaptations for Students with Disabilities

To accommodate students with physical disabilities, additional space is needed for specialized equipment, such as wheelchairs, and for aides who may accompany the students. An appropriate work area requires approximately twice the usual amount of space—that is, the equivalent of two work stations per student. Specialized equipment and furniture are also needed.

If each room has sufficient space, portable equipment and adjustable furniture can be used to make at least one work station in every room accessible to students with disabilities. Provision of adequate space requires significantly less expense than the installation of permanent equipment, which often goes unused.

Ways to ensure accessibility include
- providing braille equivalents on labels for switches and equipment
- using wire pulls on cabinets and lever-controlled faucets on sinks
- equipping any emergency eye washes with extendable hoses

All wall-mounted objects should be above base cabinets so blind students won't risk bumping into them.

The *ADA Accessibility Guidelines for Buildings and Facilities* (ADAAG) defines a number of requirements for maximum counter heights, reach ranges, and grasping and twisting limitations. For example, the ADAAG specifies that sinks used by disabled students must be no more than 17 cm (6.5 in.) deep and must be mounted to accommodate students in wheelchairs. (For adults, this would mean a counter no more than 86 cm, or 34 in. high, with a 69-centimeter or 27-inch minimum vertical knee space.)

The school district advisor should have information about local, state, and federal guidelines. The ADA, enforced through the United States Department of Justice, requires compliance with ADAAG or *Uniform Federal Accessibility Standards* (UFAS) requirements.

See Appendix E for more information on facility adaptations for students with special needs.

Other Teaching Environments

An optimal science program includes access to natural settings in which to study basic science concepts. (Be sure to include the outdoor areas for science activities in the initial facilities design plan.) The following are all desirable:
* native plants on the school grounds
* a garden
* greenhouse with water source
* storage shed for garden tools
* nature trails
* natural outdoor areas with a variety of environments
* educational kiosks

A less expensive alternative to a greenhouse is a small (1.2 m deep by 2.4 m wide, or 4 by 8 ft.) lean-to structure protruding from the wall of a science room, glazed with insulating glass, and equipped with supplementary day and night lighting and a floor drain.

"Designing Elementary School Science Facilities" was written by James T. Biehle, Inside/Out Architecture, Inc., Clayton, Missouri; Sandra S. West, Department of Biology, Southwest Texas State University, San Marcos; and LaMoine L. Motz, Oakland County Schools, Waterford, Michigan.

Editor: Suzanne Lieblich

Other contributors were Patricia S. Bowers, Center for Mathematics and Science, University of North Carolina, Chapel Hill; Terry Kwan, TK Associates, Brookline, Massachusetts; and Victor M. Showalter, Purdue University, West Lafayette, Indiana.

RESOURCES FOR THE ROAD

ADA Accessibility Guidelines for Buildings and Facilities. (1991, July 26). *Federal Register, 56* (144).

American Association for the Advancement of Science. (1991). *Barrier Free in Brief: Laboratories and Classrooms in Science and Engineering.* Washington, DC: Author.

American Chemical Society. (1995). *Safety in Academic Chemistry Laboratories* (6th ed.). Washington, DC: Author.

Biehle, James T. (1995, May). Complying with Science. *American School and University, 67* (9), 54–56. (Discusses ADA issues in science labs.)

Biehle, James T. (1995, November). Six Science Labs for the 21st Century. *School Planning and Management, 34* (9), 39–42.

Biehle, James T., Motz, LaMoine L., and West, Sandra S. (1999). *NSTA Guide to School Science Facilities.* Arlington, VA: National Science Teachers Association.

California Department of Education, Science and En- vironmental Education Unit. (1993). *Science Facilities Design for California Public Schools.* Sacramento, CA: Author.

Collins, B. Kevin. (1985, May). One Person's Trash... *Science and Children, 22* (8),17.

Dean, Robert A., Dean, Melanie Messer, Gerlovich, Jack A., and Spiglanin, Vivian. (1993). *Safety in the Elementary Science Classroom.* Arlington, VA: National Science Teachers Association.

Flinn Biological Catalog/Reference Manual. (1996). Batavia, IL: Flinn Scientific, Inc. (P.O. Box 219, Batavia, IL 60510) (Contains advice on safety in the laboratory.)

Flinn Chemical Catalog/Reference Manual. (1996). Batavia, IL: Flinn Scientific, Inc. (Contains advice on safety in the laboratory.)

Florida Department of Education. (1992). *Science Safety: No Game of Chance!* Tallahassee, FL: Author.

Florida Department of Education. (1993). *Science for All Students: The Florida Pre K–12 Science Curriculum Framework*. Tallahassee, FL: Author.

Fox, Peggy. (1994, January). Creating a Laboratory: It's Elementary. *Science and Children, 31* (4), 20–22.

Harbeck, Mary B. (1985, October). Getting the Most Out of Elementary Science. *Science and Children, 23* (2), 44–45.

Kaufman, James A. *The Kaufman Letter* (quarterly newsletter includes safety issues). Natick, MA: James A. Kaufman & Associates. (192 Worcester Road, Natick, MA 01760-2252).

Los Angeles, Orange, and San Diego County Offices of Education. (1989). *Remodeling and Building Science Instruction Facilities in Elementary, Middle, Junior, and Senior High Schools*. (1989). Downey, CA: Los Angeles County Office of Education. (Also available from Orange County Department of Education, Coast Mesa, CA, and San Diego County Office of Education, San Diego, CA.)

Madrazo, Gerry M., and **Motz, LaMoine L**. (Eds.). (1993).

Fourth Sourcebook for Science Supervisors. Arlington, VA: National Science Teachers Association.

McFee, Evan. (1985, May). A Jugful of Science. *Science and Children, 22* (8), 24.

Mione, Lawrence V. (1995). *Facilities Standards for Technology in New Jersey Schools*. Trenton, NJ: New Jersey State Department of Education.

National Science Teachers Association. (1995). Laboratory Science (Position statement). In *NSTA Handbook 1995–1996* (pp. 209–212). Arlington, VA: Author.

National Science Teachers Association. (1993). *Safety in the Elementary Science Classroom* (Rev. ed.). Arlington, VA: Author.

Public Schools of North Carolina. (1991). *North Carolina Public Schools Facility Standards: A Guide for Planning School Facilities*. Raleigh, NC: North Carolina Department of Public Instruction, School Planning.

Public Schools of North Carolina. (1992). *Furnishing and Equipment Standards: A Guide for Planning and Equipping New Facilities and Evaluating Existing Schools*. Raleigh, NC: North Carolina Department of Public Instruction, School Planning.

Reese, Kenneth M. (Ed.). (1985). *Teaching Chemistry to Physically Handicapped Students* (Rev. ed.). Washington, DC: American Chemical Society.

School Facilities Branch, Maryland State Department of Education. (1994). *Science Facilities Design Guidelines*. Baltimore, MD: Author.

Showalter, Victor M. (Ed.). (1984). *Conditions for Good Science Teaching*. Arlington, VA: National Science Teachers Association.

Six Secrets to Holding a Good Meeting Every Time (Brochure). (n.d.). Saint Paul, MN: 3M Company, Audiovisual Division.

Texas Education Agency (TEA). (1989). *Planning a Safe and Effective Science Learning Environment*. Austin, TX: Author. (Available from Publications, Distribution, and Fees Office, TEA, 1701 North Congress Avenue, Austin, TX 78701-1494.)

19 Texas Administrative Code, Chapter 61, Subchapter H (School Facilities Standards), ' 61.102. (Available from Director, School Facilities, TEA, 1701 North Congress Avenue, Austin, TX 78701-1494.)

Ward, Susan, and **West, Sandra S**. (1990, May). Accidents in Texas High School Chemistry Labs. *The Texas Science Teacher, 19* (2), 14–19.

West, Sandra S. (1991, September). Lab Safety. *The Science Teacher, 58* (9), 45–49.

Young, J. R. (1972). A Second Survey of Safety in Illinois High School Laboratories. *Journal of Chemical Education, 49* (1), 55. (Contains research on space necessary for safety in the laboratory.)

The full text to most of these resources is available on NSTA's supplementary *Resources for the Road CD-ROM*.

Appendix D
Addresses for Program Information

Biological Science Curriculum Study (BSCS)
Pikes Peak Research Park
5415 Mark Dabling Blvd.
Colorado, Springs, CO 80918-3842
TEL 719-531-5550
FAX 719-531-9104
EMAIL infor@nscs.org
http://www.bscs.org/
Science for Life and Living

Lawrence Hall of Science
University of California at Berkeley
Berkeley, CA 94720-5200

> *Chemicals, Health, Environment, and Me*
>   *(CHEM)*
> *Science Education for Public*
>   *Understanding Program (SEPUP)*
> TEL 510-642-8718
> FAX 510-642-3131
> EMAIL sepup@uclink4.berkeley.edu
> http://www.lhs.berkeley.edu/SEPUP/
>   chem.htm
>
> *Great Explorations in Math and Science*
>   *(GEMS)*
> TEL 510-642-7771
> FAX 510-642-0309
> EMAIL gems@uclink.berkeley.edu
> http://www.lhs.berkeley.edu/gems/

Education Development Center, Inc. (EDC)
55 Chapel Street
Newton, MA 02458-1060
TEL 800-793-5076
EMAIL www@edc.org
http://www.edc.org/

Life Lab Science Program
1156 High Street
Santa Cruz, CA 95064
TEL 831-459-2001
FAX 831-459-3483
EMAIL lifelab@zzyx.ucsc.edu
http://www.lifelab.org/

Delta Education, Inc.
80 Northwest Blvd.
PO Box 3000
Nashua, NH 03061-3000
TEL 800-258-1302
FAX 603-886-4632
EMAIL mbacon@delta-edu.com
http://www.delta-ed.com/scis.html
Science Curriculum Improvement Study 3
  (SCIS3+)

National Science Resources Center
955 L'Enfant Plaza, SW, Suite 8400
Washington, DC 20560-0952
TEL 202-287-2063
FAX 202-287-2070
EMAIL nsrcsite@nas.edu
http://www.si.edu/nsrc/pubs/stc/overv.htm
Science and Technology for Children (STC)

> Published and distributed by:
> Carolina Biological Supply Company
> 2700 York Road
> Burlington, NC 27215-3398
> TEL 800-334-5551
> FAX 800-222-7112
> EMAIL carolina@carolina.com
> http://www.carolina.com/stc.htm

Appendix E

Science for All: Including *Each* Student

A major theme in the *National Science Education Standards* is that science is for all students, and that all students should have the opportunity to attain high levels of scientific literacy. The purpose of this appendix is to elaborate on this theme and to offer practical suggestions for engaging a diverse student body in high-quality science education.

This appendix emphasizes working with students, such as girls, minorities, or students with disabilities, who traditionally receive unequal attention in the science classroom. We focus upon students with disabilities for two reasons. First, the move toward inclusion—educating students with disabilities in general education classrooms rather than in segregated settings—is increasingly the norm rather than the exception. Second, when we think about how to address students' disability-related needs, we often come up with approaches and curricula that help all students succeed in science.

As an early childhood educator, you are well attuned to differences among the children in your classroom. Children enter school with different experiences, background knowledge, and learning styles. Between kindergarten and sixth grade, they will undergo a number of major developmental changes, and not all children in a given grade will reach particular developmental milestones at the same time. Practices that are used in early childhood education, such as presenting information in a variety of formats, exploring topics through a variety of activities, and continual informal assessment, will serve you well in helping all students succeed.

All *Means Each and Every Student*

The focus on "all" represents a significant change in our expectations about science education and ideas about who can do science. It used to be that only a small percentage of students—usually boys, usually white, usually nondisabled—was expected to be interested and to do well in science. Now it is clear that the demands of a technological society require every person to be a capable science thinker and informed decision maker. This is why "all" means each and every student: students with disabilities as well as nondisabled students, girls as well as boys, students of color as well as white students, students from low-income families as well as from high-income families.

To ensure that each student learns science, special attention must be paid to those groups who have traditionally been underrepresented in science. We still face gaps in science participation and achievement based on such factors as gender, race and

MARY LEVIN, DO-IT PROGRAM

Diversity Among Scientists

While we remember famous Nobel Prize winners, inventors, and scientists, we often forget the tens of thousands of other scientists who are women and men of all races and ethnicities, many of whom have disabilities. Many people have heard of George Washington Carver, Marie Curie, and Stephen Hawking, but there are other notable scientists such as:

- Temple Grandin, an internationally recognized designer of livestock handling equipment. She currently serves as assistant professor of animal science at Colorado State University. Temple Grandin is autistic.
- David James, a tenured associate professor of mathematics at Howard University. He conducts research on differential topology and computer modeling and is the recipient of a Martin Luther King and Rosa Parks Visiting Professorship Award from Wayne State University in Detroit. David James is African-American and deaf.
- Geerat J. Vermeij, a preeminent evolutionary biologist and paleontologist. He is a professor at the University of California-Davis, and has been awarded MacArthur and Guggenheim fellowships. Geerat Vermeij is blind.

Teachers make an important difference

Temple Grandin, David James, and Geerat Vermeij don't fit the stereotypes of scientists and mathematicians. Part of the reason for their success is teachers—teachers who encouraged them, believed in them, and taught ways that facilitated achievement and interest.

Good teachers helped me to achieve success. I was able to overcome autism because I had good teachers. At age 2 ½ I was placed in a structured nursery school with experienced teachers.... Children with autism need to have a structured day, and teachers who know how to be firm and gentle.
—Temple Grandin (1998)

Mrs. Saplow saw to it that I became a fully responsible member of her class. Her sunny, extroverted personality created a forgiving atmosphere in which integration was natural, even inescapable. My classmates never uttered rude remarks about blindness, and the enterprising Mrs. Saplow never met a project or an activity in which I could take no part.... Full inclusion to Mrs. Saplow was not merely an empty phrase or a distant bureaucratic mandate; it was a state of mind, the manifestation of a deep conviction that the blind should be treated with equality and dignity along with everyone else.
—Geerat Vermeij (1997)

ethnicity, and disability, and we are far from having everyone achieve scientific literacy and ability.

Equity: From Access to Outcome

It was once believed that simply offering equal opportunity would make science available to everyone. The assumption was that if the door was open, students would enter, learn, and thereby end the differences in participation and achievement based on such factors as race, ethnicity, gender or disability. But students came through the door with different levels of experience and skills. Different groups of students received very different degrees of welcome.

Although opportunity is a prerequisite for learning, the *Standards* emphasize outcomes of learning. The *Standards* recognize that although important, access and treatment are not ends in themselves. The goal is that all students, independent of race, ethnicity, gender, or disability, will learn and be able to do science.

Equity means supporting students to achieve high-level outcomes. It does not mean treating all students the same. Different children learn differently and may need different instructional strategies to be successful in science. Not all students will achieve at the same level. But their differences in achievement should not be based on race, ethnicity, gender, or disability. Full access and fair treatment are important means to the end, but the process must lead to results—to achievement of the *Standards* by each student.

Start with the Strengths and Strengthen the Weaknesses

Too often, we focus on what students can't or don't do, especially when working with students with disabilities or from other groups that have traditionally been underrepresented in science. Yet all students have unique experiences and knowledge that can contribute to science learning. When we recognize this and switch our initial focus from deficit to strength, we can enhance the science experience not just for students from underrepresented groups but for all learners.

Consideration of the strengths that students bring to science should permeate all aspects of science education, including how we teach and structure classroom interactions, how we assess students, and how we select and present content. Science requires invention, innovation, and the continuous application of alternative perspectives and hypotheses. Learning environments that build on the strengths of all students will result in higher-quality education for everyone.

Building on students' strengths also means identifying where students need help or where they didn't get equal opportunities in prior education. It makes sense to compensate for the opportunities students might have been denied. For example, a girl who has not had a fair chance in the block corner in preschool may need opportunities to build with materials and learn from experience about creating stable foundations and supporting height and arches. Or a disabled student who has had less opportunity to explore on his own may need experiences that will enable him to investigate his environment.

It is not that students don't have real weaknesses to identify and address. Rather, educators must identify how students' differences or limitations affect the learning experience, instead of letting economic background or physical disability define the student.

Equity in Practice

Science for all is "easy to say, hard to do" (Malcom, 1994). Teachers are the key to creating equitable science classrooms and learning experiences for all children. The *Standards* emphasize constructivism and inquiry, which are central to equity. Building on prior knowledge and experience can help students validate their identities, and help them see the science in their lives and communities. Inquiry, combined with high-quality learning

Be Specific About Differences or Limitations

Michael, a third grader, struggles when asked to make predictions about the outcomes of events presented in stories that his teacher reads out loud. Does this mean that Michael is incapable of the higher-order thinking required for science? Not at all. It turns out that Michael—who is a keen observer of his environment and loves to draw—is fully capable of making predictions, but Michael is a visual learner and needs visual support. If the events are presented to him visually through pictures, demonstrations, or hands-on activities, he readily predicts their outcomes.

outcomes, can be a powerful tool not just for pursuing scientific questions but for helping students take charge of their own learning, assert their own views, and become strong thinkers, communicators, and actors.

Below are strategies for supporting a diverse group of students to ask questions, gather information, conduct investigations, and analyze and present findings. These suggestions are based on research and work in progress.

1. Guide students as they begin to engage in the inquiry process.

Some students may have had more encouragement, practice, and opportunity than others to ask questions, explore, and make sense of their investigations. This is because of assumptions our society makes about what different groups of people may be able to do. For example, a common misconception is that children with disabilities are unable to participate in hands-on science investigations because of their disability, which can result in the exclusion of students with disabilities from such activities. Consequently, students with disabilities may come to believe that science is something that they can't do. As another example, traditional gender socialization in some cultures rewards young girls for being neat, quiet, and not making mistakes. These messages may lead girls to believe that science investigations—which often involve getting dirty, taking intellectual risks, and challenging existing explanations—are not appropriate for them.

Such societal expectations, which counter the notion that all students can learn science, must be carefully addressed. Fostering inquiry in culturally sensitive ways may mean learning more about how members of that culture question one another and build knowledge. To help reticent students guess, hypothesize, and wonder aloud, create safe environments where contributions are encouraged. Don't allow teasing or negative sanctions to be attached to wrong or even "silly" answers.

Value the variety of approaches that children use to solve problems. There is more than one way to do science and the expansion of scientific methodologies has led to new discovery and new fields of inquiry. For example, the observation methods used by Jane Goodall and Sarah Blaffer Hrdy have changed much of what we know about primate behavior. Barbara McClintock won a Nobel Prize for her work on the DNA of corn by "listening" to her corn plants and trying to see the world from their perspective. These discoveries are often cited as evidence of how diverse perspectives and support for innovation contribute to better science.

2. Make information resources available in multiple formats.

Students differ in how they learn best. Some students learn well from lectures, some from visual media (such as pictures, graphs, videos, or diagrams), while others like to learn from text. No single format will be effective or even accessible to all students in your classroom. Every student learns better if the content is presented in multiple formats, and for some a given format is necessary to gain access to information. For example, both deaf students and hearing students who are visual learners may find images more comprehensible than verbal descriptions. Many early-childhood programs give students the opportunity to learn through pictures, by listening to stories, by acting on objects and materials, by reading, and by singing songs.

Using multiple means and media serves students with disabilities well. You can support disabled children by providing access to information in a format in which they learn best. At the same time, help students become more proficient with less ideal formats by engaging with the content and building on students' curiosity.

The Full Option Science System (FOSS) is one example of a specialized curriculum that is useful for all students. FOSS was originally designed to serve students with disabilities, well before the *Standards* were developed. As FOSS's hands-on, inquiry-based approach to science gained widespread acceptance, FOSS itself was mainstreamed and used with all students, and now is frequently recommended and used.

3. Give students opportunities to express their ideas in multiple formats.

Teachers of young students whose literacy skills are still emerging know that students' writing often provides only a limited lens on what they have learned. Using writing tasks to assess learning particularly puts at a disadvantage those students who are more artistically inclined or who have difficulty writing because of a disability. Additional options for student expression that have been used successfully in the science classroom include oral responses, audio recordings, artwork, music, drama, photography, video, and sign language. Multimedia computer programs such as *KidPix* (Broderbund) or *ClarisWorks* (Claris Corporation) also offer students multiple options for expressing ideas through images, animations, sounds, and words in limitless combinations.

4. Make the process of investigation fully accessible.

Conducting experiments, manipulating materials, and using tools are integral to science inquiry. Pay attention to physical access by choosing materials and equipment that everyone can get to and handle. Encourage exploration using different modalities to ensure that students with disabilities and students with diverse learning styles can participate in hands-on activities. If the focus is on one particular property of an object (e.g., sound), explore how this property can be described using different modalities (e.g., touch/vibration). This might allow deaf students and other students with visual learning styles to make significant contributions to this activity, and lead to interesting discussions about how one modality may not translate into another. However, do not assume a student's need for accommodation is based on a disability. Ask the students and their parents what they might need or how their comfort can be increased during an activity.

Don't exclude students from an activity because you worry that they will get distracted or hurt, or break the equipment. Take proper safety precautions (such as using protective glasses), give careful instructions, supervise, and create a calm environment when doing hands-on science with all children. If you conduct accessible learning activities, devise a way for all children to participate safely—for example, use desks and lab tables that are the right height for wheelchairs, or use science equipment that can be easily held and manipulated. Pair students as lab or classroom partners and they can build relationships to support each other's strengths and needs.

Accessible Tools and Equipment

The following resources provide information about science tools and equipment that are accessible to students with disabilities.

American Association for the Advancement of Science (AAAS). (1991). *Laboratories and Classrooms in Science and Engineering.* Washington, DC: Author.

Barrier Free Education, <http://barrier-free.arch.gatech.edu/>. Georgia Tech's Barrier Free Education Web site is a resource site helping students with disabilities gain access to math and science education. The site is intended to inform and assist students with disabilities, and their parents and teachers.

Underrepresented Groups

The following resources provide information about scientists and mathematicians from underrepresented groups.

American Association for the Advancement of Science (AAAS). (1996). *Stepping into the Future: African-Americans in Science and Engineering.* Washington, DC: Author.

Lakes-Matyas, Marsha and **Haley-Oliphant, Ann** (Eds.) (1996). *Women Life Scientists: Past, Present, and Future.* Bethesda, MD: American Physiological Society.

Lang, Harry G. (1994). *Silence of the Spheres: The Deaf Experience in the History of Science.* Westport, CT: Bergin & Garvey.

Lang, Harry G. and **Meath-Lang, Bonnie.** (1995*). Deaf Persons in the Arts and Sciences: A Bibliographical Dictionary.* Westport, CT: Greenwood Press.

Stern, Virginia W. and **Summers, Laureen.** (Eds.) (1995). *AAAS Resource Directory of Scientists and Engineers with Disabilities.* Washington, DC: American Association for the Advancement of Science.

Triana, Estrella M., Abbruzzese, Anne, and **Matyas, Marsha L.** (Eds.) (1992). *Stepping into the Future: Hispanics in Science and Engineering.* Washington, DC: American Association for the Advancement of Science.

Vermeij, Geerat J. (1998). *Privileged Hands.* New York: W. H. Freeman & Co.

Woods, Michael, with **Blumenkopf, Todd A., et al.** (Eds.) (1997). *Working Chemists with Disabilities: Expanding Opportunities in Science.* Washington, DC: American Chemical Society.

Internet resources
Deaf and Hard of Hearing Professionals in Science
http://www.gallaudet.edu/~mssdsci/rolemodels.html

Women in Science
http://library.thinkquest.org/20117/

African Americans in Science
http://www.lib.lsu.edu/lib/chem/display/faces.html

Accessible Software and Web Sites

The following organizations have information for educators about accessible design of computer software and Web sites:

Center for Applied Special Technology (CAST)
39 Cross Street, Suite 201
Peabody, MA 01960
TEL 978-531-8555
TTY 978-538-3110
FAX 978-531-0192
EMAIL: cast@cast.org
http://www.cast.org/

CAST is an educational, not-for-profit organization that uses technology to expand opportunities for all people, including those with disabilities. Available through its Web site is Bobby, a Web-based tool that analyzes Web pages for their accessibility to people with disabilities.

The CPB/WGBH National Center for Accessible Media (NCAM)
WGBH Educational Foundation
125 Western Avenue
Boston, MA 02134
TEL/TTY 617-300-3400
FAX 617-300-1035
EMAIL ncam@wgbh.org
http://www.wgbh.org/wgbh/pages/ncam/

NCAM is a research and development facility that works to make media accessible to underserved populations such as people with disabilities, speakers of minority languages, and people with low literacy skills. This Web site includes guidelines for evaluating software and Web sites for accessibility to people with disabilities.

Equal Access to Software and Information (EASI)
Rochester Institute of Technology
c/o Teaching, Learning & Technology Group
PO Box 18928
Rochester, NY 14618
TEL 716-244-9065
EMAIL easi@tltgroup.org
http://www.rit.edu/~easi/

The EASI Web site is a resource to the education community by providing information and guidance in the area of access-to-information technologies by individuals with disabilities. It includes information about how to evaluate Web sites for accessibility.

5. Make role models available.

Role models allow students to see their own concerns reflected in science and math, and can help develop students' interest in these disciplines. Provide students with opportunities to learn about the contributions of scientists and mathematicians from under-represented groups. Use materials in which the stories, examples, and images reflect diversity; avoid stereotypes. Seek out teachers, scientists, or mathematicians from under-represented groups as resources for your classroom.

6. Use technology that is accessible for all.

Select technology programs and online resources that are age appropriate and accessible to students with disabilities. Increasingly, technology products developed for the general population also provide access for disabled users. For example, some word processors now include features such as text-to-speech and word prediction that support students who have difficulties reading and writing or students who are blind. An increasing number of Web sites are accessible to disabled users. But don't take accessibility for granted—new innovations in technology sometimes unwittingly exclude some while including others. For example, the computer mouse makes computer use easier for people who never learned touch-typing, but more difficult for people with cerebral palsy. Similarly, icon-based computer systems were first heralded as more user-friendly than conventional systems, but icon-based systems exclude blind users because these systems don't allow text-to-speech translation.

To identify programs or Web sites that can be used by all students in your class, including those with disabilities, look for icons that identify a program or Web site as accessible. You can also use Bobby, a program by the Center for Applied Special Technology. Bobby allows users to test Web sites for accessibility for disabled users. While this program doesn't ensure complete accessibility, it can help you identify major access barriers, such as the lack of text descriptions for images and other graphics. Blind users rely on such descriptions to access information.

7. Make assistive technology available when necessary.

Assistive technology, such as touch screens, alternate keyboards, switches, head-mounted pointers, word-prediction software, voice input and output technology, and caption decoders may be critical to enhance some students' participation and capacity.

Don't use assistive technologies to compensate for inadequacies in the curriculum but couple technologies with a curriculum that is accessible to all. For example, don't set up a curriculum that relies heavily on print-only media because a blind student can access that information only through Braille. Instead, use more electronic media—with described images and text that can be read out loud—to change the way information is presented.

Assistive technologies can benefit nondisabled as well as disabled students. For example, while closed captions provide deaf students with access to narration, dialogue, and other sounds in television and video programs, captions also can improve the comprehension of video material for hearing students. Try to make assistive devices available to all so that the technology doesn't set students with disabilities apart, and so every student benefits from the technology.

8. Emphasize cooperation and collaboration.

Have students work in mixed-ability groups where each student can use his or her strengths. Students will need your help and guidance to become independent learners and to build a community of learners among themselves. You may need to engineer the groups to balance talents that complement one another. You may also need to give attention to group processes, such as the roles played by different group members and the experiences students have within these groups. Make sure that all students are actively involved and are rotating roles, so that, for example, the girls aren't always observing while the boys manipulate materials.

Professional Development for Equity

We can prepare ourselves through information and resources to support every child's achievement. Learn how to create accessible learning environments for your students, how to use materials and technology that are accessible to everyone, how to use teaching strategies to address diverse students' needs, and how to use methods and strategies for informal and formal assessment.

You don't have to go far to learn these skills. Take advantage of what your colleagues know, and form cross-disciplinary teams. Seek out colleagues, both within your immediate school community and in the wider education and scientific communities, and build informal and formal collaborations. Form partnerships that include other elementary school teachers, special educators, science specialists, equity experts, and colleagues or experts from underrepresented groups. Collaborative teaching arrangements that involve special education and general education teachers can be especially effective. (See pages 14–18 for further suggestions on professional development and the *Standards*.)

Early childhood teachers often have useful strategies that translate well into the elementary science classroom. The early childhood classroom is typically set up with stations where children have choices about what to do and what materials to use. The materials are arranged to be easily accessible to the children—at the right height, labeled with symbols or language that the child can understand, and organized to reflect and communicate some system of classification. Children have ownership of the room and the materials and are able to initiate activities and

Assistive Technology

The following organizations have more information about assistive technology.

ABLEDATA
8401 Colesville Road, Suite 200
Silver Spring, MD 20910
TEL 800-227-0216
TTY 301-608-8912
FAX 301-608-8958
EMAIL adaigle@aol.com
http://www.abledata.com/

ABLEDATA is a national database of assistive technology and rehabilitation equipment.

Alliance for Technology Access (ATA)
2175 East Francisco Boulevard, Suite L
San Rafael, CA 94901
TEL 415-455-4575
TTY 415-455-0491
FAX 415-455-0654
EMAIL atainfo@ataccess.org
http://www.ataccess.org/

ATA is a national network of community technology centers that provide information and support services to children and adults with disabilities. ATA offers training and hands-on opportunities to use assistive technology.

National Center to Improve Practice (NCIP)
c/o Education Development Center
55 Chapel Street
Newton, MA 02160
TEL 617-969-7100
http://www2.edc.org/NCIP/

NCIP promotes the effective use of technology to enhance educational outcomes for students with sensory, cognitive, physical and social/emotional disabilities. The NCIP Web site includes information about the use of technology for students with disabilities.

Rehabilitation Engineering and Assistive Technology Society of North America (RESNA)
Technical Assistance Project
1700 North Moore Street, Suite 1540
Arlington, VA 22209
TEL 703-524-6686
TTY 703-524-6639
FAX 703-524-6630
EMAIL info@resna.org
http://www.resna.org/

RESNA is an interdisciplinary association of people with an interest in technology and disability. Its purpose is to improve the potential of people with disabilities to achieve their goals through the use of technology. Contact RESNA to locate the Assistive Technology Project in your state. These projects provide information about purchasing and using assistive technology.

Trace Research and Development Center
University of Wisconsin-Madison
5901 Research Park Boulevard
Madison, WI 53719-1252
TEL 608-262-6966
TTY 608-263-5408
FAX 608-262-8848
EMAIL web@trace.wisc.edu
http://www.trace.wisc.edu/

The Trace Center at the University of Wisconsin-Madison is a research and development facility that focuses on making information technologies more accessible for everyone through the process known as universal, or accessible, design. The Center's Web site contains a wealth of information about accessible design and assistive technology.

pursue open-ended investigation. In turn, teachers can observe the children's inquiry and support investigations through questions that are directly related to the questions children are pursuing at the moment. From there, teachers may be able to identify what a child knows and what question or activity might take the student to the next level of understanding.

In the same way, we can draw on lessons from early-intervention specialists who work with young children with developmental disabilities. These specialists are attuned to the developmental steps in a given learning task, and are able to break things down into component parts. They focus on supporting physical as well as cognitive development, and their classrooms are often set up to encourage children to use their senses fully, even if one or more of those senses is impaired. Activities reinforce basic concepts such as cause-and-effect (e.g., using busyboxes, pushing an object off a table and watching it fall, building a structure and knocking it down, exploring object permanence), and the idea that something exists even when it is hidden from view (e.g., peekaboo and other hiding games). Most children develop these understandings in the first years of life, but children with developmental delays may need help making the connections between the physical world and cognitive identification. In both cases, these concepts are essential to understanding science.

In addition to collaborating with your school district and local universities, you can get information and participate in professional development opportunities through a variety of national organizations. The organizations listed to the right offer information, resources, and workshops on how to engage underrepresented groups in science and mathematics education. Many resources and workshops are available on the Internet.

Student Assessment

Assessment is a key aspect of teaching and learning in an inquiry classroom. It is also central to teaching a diverse group of students. Assessment ensures that learning builds on prior understanding—which may differ from student to student—and that students actually acquire the desired knowledge and skills.

Informal and formal assessments of individual students help you determine whether the needs of each student are addressed, and if all students are making progress towards the learning goals outlined in the *Standards*. Check that the assessments themselves are unbiased and equitable. The following strategies can help you make assessments.

Engaging Underrepresented Groups in Science Education

The following organizations provide information, resources, and professional development opportunities on how to engage underrepresented groups in science education:

American Association for the Advancement of Science (AAAS)
Education and Human Resources Program
1200 New York Avenue, NW
Washington, DC 20005
TEL 202-326-6400
EMAIL webmaster@aaas.org
http://www.aaas.org/

AAAS disseminates print and Internet materials on equity in science education, including materials from the Collaboration for Equity. These materials help teachers delve more deeply into how to create equitable environments and curricula, provide workshop designs and professional development activities, and offer tips for moving equity into the mainstream. AAAS' Roadmaps and Rampways project examines the factors that have influenced the career paths of disabled students in science, engineering and technology.

Disabilities, Opportunities, Internetworking & Technology (DO-IT)
University of Washington
Box 354842
Seattle, WA 98195-4842
TEL/TTY 206-685-DOIT (3648)
FAX 206-221-4171
EMAIL doit@u.washington.edu
http://www.washington.edu/doit/

The DO-IT Program at the University of Washington serves to increase the participation of individuals with disabilities in challenging academic programs and careers, and promotes the use of computer and networking technologies to increase independence, productivity, and participation of people with disabilities in education and employment. DO-IT sponsors programs and delivers presentations and workshops to enhance the lives of people with disabilities throughout the world. DO-IT activities are hosted at conferences, universities, K–12 schools, corporations, state agencies, and professional organizations. DO-IT Internet resources are designed to facilitate communication and provide access to information.

Engaging Underrepresented Groups in Science Education

The Center for Curriculum Innovation
Lawrence Hall of Science (LHS)
University of California at Berkeley
Berkeley, CA 94720-5200
TEL 510-642-1823
EMAIL lhsinfo@uclink.berkeley.edu
http://www.lhs.berkeley.edu/centers.html

The Center for Curriculum Innovation develops instructional materials and professional development methods that translate experience, research, theory, and the *Standards* into exciting learning experiences. LHS programs, including EQUALS, Family Math, FOSS, GEMS, and MARE, provide ongoing support through innovative materials and methods.

The Council for Exceptional Children (CEC)
1920 Association Drive
Reston, VA 20191-1589
TEL 1-888-CEC-SPED (232-7733)
TTY 703-264-9446
FAX 703-264-9494
EMAIL cec@cec.sped.org
http://www.cec.sped.org/

CEC is an international professional organization dedicated to improving educational outcomes for students with disabilities and the gifted. It disseminates information about teaching exceptional students through its Web site, print and video materials, and annual conference. CEC also offers opportunities for continuing education through online and onsite workshops.

The Education Trust
1725 K Street, Suite 200
Washington, DC 20006
TEL 202-293-1217
FAX 202-293-2605
http://www.edtrust.org/

The Education Trust promotes high academic achievement for all students, kindergarten through college. The Education Trust disseminates information about *Standards*-based education for underrepresented groups through print, the Web, and conferences.

Eisenhower National Clearinghouse (ENC)
1929 Kenny Road
Columbus, OH 43210-1079
TEL 800-621-5785
FAX 614-292-2066
EMAIL info@enc.org
http://www.enc.org/

ENC's mission is to identify effective curriculum resources, create high-quality professional development materials, and disseminate information and products to improve K–12 mathematics and science teaching and learning. ENC is funded by the U.S. Department of Education's Office of Educational Research and Improvement.

The National Center on Accessing the General Curriculum
Center for Applied Special Technology (CAST)
39 Cross Street, Suite 201
Peabody, MA 01960
TEL 978-531-8555
TTY 978-538-3110
FAX 978-531-0192
EMAIL: cast@cast.org
http://www.cast.org/

The National Center on Accessing the General Curriculum is funded by the U.S Department of Education and is a collaboration of the Harvard University Children's Initiative/Harvard Law School, Boston College, CAST, and CEC. The goals of the Center are to build a unified knowledge base and to develop and disseminate a new vision and practical approaches for providing disabled students with access to the general curriculum.

Science Education for Students with Disabilities (SESD)
c/o Judy Egelston-Dodd, President
Office of Faculty & Staff Development
National Technical Institutes for the Deaf at RIT
52 Lomb Memorial Drive
Rochester, NY 14623
TEL 716-475-6932
FAX 716-475-6400
http://www.as.wvu.edu/~scidis/organizations/
    sepd_main.html

SESD promotes and advances the teaching of science and the development of curricula and instructional materials for disabled students at all levels. SESD publishes *The Journal of Science for Persons with Disabilities*, hosts annual meetings in conjunction with the conventions of the National Science Teachers Association, and co-sponsors a teacher of the year award in science education for students with disabilities.

The Women's Educational Equity Act (WEEA) Equity Resource Center
Education Development Center
55 Chapel Street
Newton, MA 02458-1060
TEL 800-225-3088
TTY 800-354-6798
FAX 617-332-4318
EMAIL weeactr@edc.org
http://www.edc.org/WomensEquity/

WEEA Equity Resource Center works to improve educational, social, and economic outcomes for women and girls. The WEEA Center disseminates print materials, offers online workshops, and manages the Educational Equity Discussion List (EDEQUITY), an international electronic discussion about all aspects of educational equity.

1. Don't infer what students can do based on their group membership.

It is important to understand the obstacles and differential opportunities faced by some groups so that you can counter societal stereotypes and discrimination. Your knowledge of which groups a student belongs to can help you in your informal assessments, but don't automatically attribute group characteristics to an individual. Base your decisions about what learning experience a student should have on what the student brings to the classroom, not on assumptions about his or her group membership.

There are no "one size fits all" approaches to learning. Different instructional strategies will work with different students. Constant observation of what students bring to the classroom, and continuous analysis of where students are in relation to the desired learning goals, can help to ensure that each student's needs are met.

2. Include all students in assessments.

The only way to gauge if all students achieve the learning goals outlined in the *Standards* is to have all students participate in the assessment. Yet students with disabilities are often "excused" from assessments. As a result, teachers don't have an accurate picture of students' learning and can't draw conclusions about student progress or ensure that the appropriate educational entity—class, school, district, or government—is meeting its obligations for educating all children.

It is true that some national, state, and district assessments may not be appropriate or valid measures of *Standards*-based science learning for all students. Tests should be accessible, unbiased, and valid, but they often are not. Until tests are accessible for all students, we should consider how to provide accommodations and help the child with testing to provide a foundation of good information from which to take action.

3. Use assessment methods that are accessible for all students.

In your own classroom, there is much you can do to include all students in assessment. Give students a number of ways to show what they have learned. Encourage students to develop hands-on demonstrations, write narratives, put on plays, make recordings, create artwork, use photography and video, and design multimedia reports on the computer. Take clues from these presentations about what enables different students to show off their knowledge, and construct assessments that give students choices of materials and approaches.

Accommodate students for whom the assessment cannot be made accessible, by providing assistive technology or more time. Teachers often worry that accommodations such as extra time on a test are unfair, but extra time is fair unless the test measures how quickly a student can complete a science task. The accommodations simply make it possible for every student to demonstrate what he or she knows and is able to do.

Selecting Content

The context in which you put the science content, the way you choose what topics to focus on, and the relationship of the "nature of the learner" to the choice and delivery of content are key considerations in reaching all students.

1. Recognize variation in the "nature of the learner."

As an educator who works with children in the elementary grades, you are well aware of the many developmental changes taking place in children between the ages of 5 and 11. Development takes place on many different levels and encompasses physical, social, emotional, and cognitive changes, for disabled and nondisabled students. Development is influenced by many factors including socialization, experiences, resources, opportunity, and the child's individual physical makeup.

As you select curriculum topics and methods, consider that your class may have students who are different from or do things differently than as predicted by the standard developmental schema.

Students may be at very different levels of capacity on key science concepts such as cause-and-effect, or key science skills such as inquiry. Cause-and-effect is an abstract concept, and children who are concrete thinkers, who have developmental disabilities, or have less experience observing physical phenomena may benefit from physical prompts and explicit connections, even as you encourage an open-ended exploration process.

Similarly, consider how to make the inquiry process available to all students. Some children have more experience guessing and imagining "what will happen if..." Part of this depends on students' grasp of how the past, present, and future differ, and their ability to project an action in their minds into some future time. Some children will benefit by permission to wonder out loud and pursue their own path, while other students will get stuck on the first step. Try scaffolding the experience—what if you start with this? And add this? And try that?

Sometimes children answer a different question from the one they were asked. Try asking the question that they answered. This can affirm their thinking, and also help children to see the connections between questions and answers. This connection may be especially important for children who have trouble answering "why" questions (perhaps because they are not ready for that level of abstraction or generalization) or "when" questions (because their sense of past, present, and future is not yet well developed).

2. Capitalize on different ways of perceiving the physical world.

Our perspective on the physical world is determined by where we stand and sit, by how we see, hear, and touch, and how we translate those experiences into general constructs. Altering our perspective provides additional insights into our understanding, and good scientific method advises us to look at the world from different angles, to turn questions and ideas upside down, and to verify our observations in multiple ways. The range of different experiences, perspectives, and interests represented in a diverse classroom can help to enhance science learning for everyone.

People with disabilities often devise innovative ways of exploring materials and their environment with senses, parts of the body, and creative instruments. Wheelchair users may have a different perspective than those who view the world by standing. Similarly, rolling in a wheelchair rather than walking can foster an intuitive important understanding of gravity, speed, and friction.

3. Support students to pursue questions that particularly intrigue them.

NSTA Pathways to the Science Standards emphasizes building on a child's prior interests and understandings. These interests and understandings are influenced not just by the child's individual characteristics, but also by demographic factors such as culture, socioeconomic status, race, ethnicity, and gender.

Children make sense of the world with the tools and resources available to them. All cultures have systematic ways of interpreting the meaning of the physical world, or classifying and understanding scientific phenomena. The explanations and concepts students are introduced to through the *Standards* may support or contrast with their own ways of organizing the world. The more you understand the origin of a student's ideas, the better you can construct a science experience that takes advantage of the student's background knowledge.

Identifying a question worth pursuing is a key science skill. Encourage each child to articulate questions within a topic about which he or she wants to know more. Value each question as a reflection of the child's prior experience and background. Help children to go beyond their worldviews, to embrace questions by peers and you. It may not always be possible to find questions in which every student in your class will be interested, and a particular student's interest may not be perfectly addressed in every inquiry you undertake. But over the course of the school year, seek a balance so that each student has the opportunity to make personal connections to science.

4. Allow for multiple entry points and a flexible content sequence.

There may not be one linear sequence that will work for all of your students. Based on the unique experiences, abilities, and prior understandings that students bring to the classroom, they may need different entry points. Try to keep the instructional sequence

Equity in Science Education

The following materials have been developed to enhance equity in science education. They provide teaching strategies, assessments, and ideas for problems and themes to investigate with your students.

Eisenhower National Clearinghouse. (1998). Multicultural Approaches in Math and Science. *ENC Focus for Mathematics and Science Education*, 5 (1).

George, Yolanda S., Malcom, Shirley M., and **Worthington, Valerie L.** (Eds.) (1995). *In Touch with Preschool.* Washington, DC: American Association for the Advancement of Science.

George, Yolanda S., Sosa, Maria, and **Bowden, Gaynelle.** (Eds.) (1997). *In Touch with Community Service Learning: A Guide to Hands-on Science.* Washington, DC: American Association for the Advancement of Science.

Lawrence Hall of Science. (1987). *Full Option Science System (FOSS).* Chicago: Encyclopedia Britannica Educational Corporation.

Matyas, Marsha L. and **Triana, Estrella M.** (Eds.) (1995). *In Touch with Electricity.* Washington, DC: American Association for the Advancement of Science.

Matyas, Marsha L. and **Triana, Estrella M.** (Eds.) (1995). *In Touch with Magnetism.* Washington, DC: American Association for the Advancement of Science.

Matyas, Marsha L. and **Triana, Estrella M.** (Eds.) (1995). *In Touch with Mathematics.* Washington, DC: American Association for the Advancement of Science.

Rethinking Schools. (1994). *Rethinking Our Classrooms: Teaching for Equity and Justice.* Milwaukee, WI: Author.

Shulman, Judith H., and **Mesa-Bains, Amalia.** (1993). *Diversity in the Classroom: A Casebook for Teachers and Teacher Educators.* Hillsdale, NJ: Research for Better Schools and Lawrence Erlbaum Association.

Sprung, Barbara, Froschl, Merle, and **Colon, Linda.** (1997). *Playtime is Science: An Equity-Based Parent/Child Science Program.* New York: Educational Equity Concepts.

Stern, Valerie, et al. (1998). *Access Science: Themes and Variations.* Washington, DC: American Association for the Advancement of Science.

Tunstall Margaret E., and **Matyas, Marsha L.** (Eds.) (1995). *In Touch with Girls and Science.* Washington, DC: American Association for the Advancement of Science.

flexible and provide multiple opportunities to approach a given science topic. This is not easy to do in a class of 30 or more diverse students, but consider strategies such as using computer and online explorations and setting up learning stations with hands-on activities that students can use independently.

Programs and Systems that Support all Learners

The program standards emphasize what has been discussed throughout this appendix: that a good program is designed around student knowledge, skills, and attitudes, that inquiry is key, and that diverse learners should have equal resources and opportunity to learn. Developing an equitable and coherent program requires a coordinated effort involving all parts of the educational enterprise.

Teachers play critical roles within this larger effort. As an innovator and program developer at the classroom and school level, you are building a repertory of strategies that work with a broad range of students and that can be shared with other teachers, parents, administrators, and policymakers. You know what makes a diverse classroom work, and you can advocate for adequate resources, assistive technology, collaborative planning time, and attention in every part of the educational system to meet the needs of all learners.

A teacher's most important role may be as program evaluator to assess progress in creating a high-quality learning environment for all students. A teacher's goal is to determine what works for whom: what approaches are effective with which students? Are there differences in participation and achievement by group membership? Ideally, these measures will be connected to similar, data-based efforts at the school, district, and state levels. Such efforts can guide decisions about curriculum, teaching, professional development, and assessment. These decisions are based not on their effectiveness for average students, but on their effectiveness for different groups of students, and ultimately for all students.

In a school providing high-quality education, demographics should not determine outcomes. If students' achievement can be predicted by variables such as residency or family income, then the system is not treating students fairly and must be changed.

We must continue to dismantle these artificial barriers to participation and achievement. This part may be easier said than done. But it is essential to preparing today's children for the scientific and technological challenges of the twenty-first century, and for ensuring the health of science education and the scientific enterprise.

"Science for All: Including *Each* Student" was written by Babette Moeller and Ellen Wahl, Education Development Center, Newton, Massachusetts.

Other contributors were Louisa Anderson and Eric Jolly, Education Development Center; Nathan Bell and Yolanda George, American Assocation for the Advancement of Science, Washington, DC; Patricia Campbell, Campbell-Kibler Associates, Groton, Massachusetts; Sami Kahn, Rutgers University, Rutgers, New Jersey; and Harilyn Rousso, Disabilities Unlimited, New York, NY.

RESOURCES FOR THE ROAD

Grandin, Temple. (2000). *My Experiences with Visual Thinking, Sensory Problems, and Communication Difficulties*. Salem, OR: Center for the Study of Autism. Available at <http://www.autism.org/temple/visual.html>.

Grandin, Temple. (2000). *Teaching Tips for Children and Adults with Autism*. Salem, OR: Center for the Study of Autism. Available at <http://www.autism.org/temple/tips.html>.

Malcom, Shirley M. (1994). Science for All: Easy to Say, Hard to Do. In A. Pendergast, ed., *In Pursuit of Excellence: National Standards for Science Education. Proceedings of the 1992 AAAS Forum for School Science*. Washington, DC: American Association for the Advancement of Science.

Vermeij, Geerat J. (1998). *Privileged Hands*. New York: W. H. Freeman & Co.